KARL KERÉNYI

HERMES

GUIDE OF SOULS

The Mythologem of the Masculine Source of Life

Translated from German by Murray Stein

Spring Publications, Inc.
Dallas, Texas

Acknowledgments for quotations from other authors have been made in the appropriate places in the text by the translator. The translation was made from *Hermes der Seelenführer*, Albae Vigilae I, Rhein Verlag, Zürich, 1944. Gabriella Lautenberg, David L. Miller, Robert Hinshaw, and James Hillman assisted in the production of the final text.

The figure of Hermes on the cover has been taken from the inside bottom of an attic red-figured bowl in the British Museum (E 58. Von Makron; Beazly *ARV*² 467, 133, and as published by Stella, *Mitologia Greca*, p. 93, bottom). The cover was designed by Doris Oesch.

2/95

Dunquin Series No. 7

Third Printing 1987

Published by Spring Publications, Inc.; P.O. Box 222069;
Dallas, Texas 75222. Printed in the United States of America

International Distributors   10.00

Spring; Postfach; 8800 Thalwil; *Switzerland*.
Japan Spring Sha, Inc.; 1–2–4, Nishisakaidani-Cho;
Ohharano, Nishikyo-Ku; Kyoto, 610–11; *Japan*.
Element Books Ltd; Longmead Shaftesbury;
Dorset SP7 8PL; *England*.

Library of Congress Cataloging-in-Publication Data

Kerényi, Karl, 1897–1973.
    Hermes, guide of souls.

    (Dunquin series ; no. 7)
    Translation of: Hermes der Seelenführer.
    Bibliography: p.
    1. Hermes (Greek deity) I. Title.
BL820.M5K413   1986   292'.211   85–18263
ISBN 0–88214–207–0

C.1

CONTENTS

A Prefatory Note...

A few words of introduction to this book may cast some light on the
place of this Hermes monograph in the biographical context of its author.
To do more than this would be pretentious, because Karl Kerényi himself
would certainly have presented his own preface with his ideas about the
God Hermes not only in regard to this book, but also in respect to further
implications from evidence accumulated through the last three decades since
this work was first conceived. Probably, for such a preface, he would have
seized an idea he was hinting at in the Introduction to his correspondence
with Thomas Mann, when he added the "Hermetic" as a third configuration
to the dualism of Apollonian and Dionysian which Nietzsche introduced
into modern cultural history. Kerényi understood the "Hermetic" as "a
specific quality in the nature, achievements, and life patterns of mankind,
as well as of the corresponding traits of roguery to be found on the surface
of man's world."[1]

When, in a letter to Kerényi, Thomas Mann wrote: "Hermes, my favourite
divinity" (p. 48 in their correspondence), he was obviously alluding to his
partner's predilection for the same God. Kerényi's hesitation in elaborating
his lecture on Hermes — held in 1942 at Eranos and not written down until
one year later — into a volume like the ones *Prometheus, Dionysos, Asklepios,
Zeus and Hera* in his series "Archetypal Images in Greek Religion,"[2] may be
owing to the fact that he felt Hermes to be so closely involved with his life,
for he recognized the continuous presence and effects of this divinity.

His special personal relation to Hermes derived from the *journey* as the
essential support of his life and his work. In the Preface to his "Unwillkür-
liche Kunstreisen,"[3] Kerényi wrote: "This book is thoroughly committed
to the Hermetic element of journey and life, to its surprises... ." But these
words are valid not only for that book. Finding and losing belong to the

ambivalent sphere of the "God of journey" who so often put into Kerényi's hand just the right reading material for a voyage. But Hermes could also reveal his presence through contrariness, as we can read in Kerényi's diary in the notation for April 1, 1952:

> ...in the Isthmus Canal. The first time it was with Anatole France's *Révolte des Anges* in a Greek translation, of which, twenty-five years ago, Miss Geroulanos, sister of the *propriétaire* [the landowner of Trachones, near Athens, I. M. Geroulanos who is often mentioned in the diary during the fifties] said with astonishment: "it is written exactly as one speaks." And now it is precisely Anatole France — in a not-as-good translation of *Thais* — that was again stolen from me, disappeared together with the chair I had reserved... Does Hermes wish to play the same game with me again? In any event I am left with the feeling of being stolen from, something uncanny, a vague sense of change in circumstances — truly something hermetic.[4]

Hermaion, a gift of Hermes, meant for Kerényi that a book or an article unexpectedly appeared at hand in the right moment, even independently of traveling. His Hermes lecture, on August 4, 1942, played an important part in his life, quite concretely favouring a crucial journey: the appreciation of this lecture in the Swiss press facilitated permission to leave Hungary and then later to establish himself definitely in the free world.

He seems to have rendered homage to this *daimon* of his fate, in 1952, during his first post-war visit in Delphi. There he walked each day to the site where, according to his intuition, Hermes used to be worshipped, even though, as a classical scholar, he was led to Delphi for the sake of its chief divinities, Apollo and Dionysos. Exactly there is the point — geographically as well as metaphorically — where personal life leads into work, in this case to Hermes Psychopompos.

Kerényi expressed it in a meditation about the "Angels" of Rilke: the poet had experienced the "Angels" — according to Kerényi — as a spiritual place without the usual boundaries which separate importance from unimportance. *"Such a place* [Kerényi's meditation continues] *can be assumed also in the sanctuary of a God of antiquity, for instance in that of Hermes. Apparently this was the case with my Hermes, Guide of Souls... ."*[5]

A direct account of the genesis of the present work is to be found in a letter dated Nov. 11, 1942, to Frau Hermann Hesse:

> The world of Hermes has been holding me captive ever since my lecture until the day before yesterday, and you will be amazed how much it grew and ripened, since its conception in the lecture — an unexpected and passively received conception, into its final, and even for myself, surprising shape.[6]

In the summer of 1943 the Hermes Lecture was published in the *Eranos-Jahrbuch* IX. A second edition, from which this translation was made, appeared as a monograph in 1944 as Number One of the new series "Albae Vigiliae,"[7] "because I felt compelled to publish it for reasons related to my situation after breaking 'official' connections with Hungary."[8] Then began the difficult existence of the free, private scholar, although interwoven and protected by Hermes.

Kerényi died on April 14, 1973, exactly on the day when thirty years of exile were completed. His grave in Ascona bears the inscription — mentioned on one of the last pages of this volume — which had been used on the isle of Imbros for those "initiated into the Mysteries of Hermes:" *tetelesmenoi Hermei.*

It was not possible for Karl Kerényi to place his favorite divinity into the series of archetypal monographs on the Gods, but one is grateful to those who have helped the figure of "the speech-gifted mediator and psychogogue" to become, in the fresh vestments of the English language, "for all to whom life is an adventure — whether an adventure of love or of spirit — ... the common guide."

Ascona, January 19, 1976.　　　　　*Magda Kerényi*

vi

PART ONE

THE HERMES OF CLASSICAL TRADITION

1 *The "Hermes Idea"*

The question that we are seeking to answer, most simply put, is this: what appeared to the Greeks as Hermes? We are not asking this question in order to elicit immediately the simplest answer, namely, "a God." To most people this would say nothing, or, at best, something highly questionable. By formulating the question as we have, we are assuming only that the name Hermes corresponds to something, to a reality, at least to a reality of the soul, but possibly to one with more inclusive implications. In this way the question does not become a wholly non-historical one, but at the same time it does not remain a purely historical one either. One must recognize the historical fact that for the Greeks their God Hermes was not a mere nothing, as he is for contemporary man; nor was he a formless power. He was something very precise, and, at least since the time of Homer, he possessed a distinctly delineated personality. As a person, though, he never displayed the arbitrariness of a mere power; he

1

was always much more contained by the definition of his own inherent meaning. It is our task as historians to represent this Hermes in his irreducible, highly personal totality.

Our inquiry passes beyond historical questions, however, if we seek to rediscover the reality borne by the Greek name Hermes in the realm of timeless reality that is not conditioned by history. The superficial appearances of the Gods' epiphanies are conditioned by time and place, of course. But no Deity can be reduced completely to color of skin, hairdressing, clothing, and other attributes without something being left over. This "left over" part is precisely what we are looking for. To find this we must obviously rely on the results of historical research, but also beyond that on a scientific understanding of major mythology.

Closely connected to the first question ("What appeared to the Greeks as Hermes? ") is a second: how could just this appear to the Greeks as God? We will not be occupying ourselves for the moment with this question, although one must not forget it altogether. It is necessary to ask this question all the more earnestly if one believes he has found the "original" Hermes in something gross and inferior. It is precisely this omission that makes most of the hypotheses about origins no more than mere unscientific conjectures. We should, however, not presume that the "something" which constitutes a God's reality must necessarily correspond to something sublime, and which according to our concepts — based precisely on the most recent conceptions of the Greek Gods — is inherent in the Hellenic God-idea. Otherwise we will fall into the error of Walter F. Otto,[1] that great scholar of Greek religion, who in the most brilliant pages he ever wrote describes Hermes as a Deity whose idea is obvious to us, and at the same time separates him from primitive aspects of his configuration — aspects that the Greeks themselves never found incompatible with his Godhood.

"Whatever may have been thought of Hermes in primitive times," we read at the conclusion of Otto's superb portrait of Hermes, "he must once have struck the eye as a brilliant flash out of the depths, that it saw a world in the God, and the God in the whole world. This is the origin of the figure of Hermes, which Homer recognized and which later generations held fast to." A Hermes-world is supposed to have been revealed to the Greeks — perhaps during that lofty period whose highest and possibly also last form of expression was the Homeric epic — a realm and domain having a place among the other domains of the world-as-a-whole, yet forming a unified totality in its own right, "the realm whose divine image is Hermes." This realm is characterized and held together by a specific logic: "It is a world in the full sense which Hermes animates and rules, a complete world, and not some fragment of the sum total of existence. All things belong to it, but they appear in a different light than in the realms of the other Gods. What occurs in it comes as though from heaven and entails no obligations; what is done in it is a virtuoso performance, where enjoyment is without responsibility. Whoever wants this world of winning gains and the favor of its God Hermes must also accept losing; the one is never without the other." Hermes is therefore "the spirit of a form of existence which under various conditions always reappears and knows both gain and loss, both shows kindness and takes pleasure in misfortune. Though much of this must appear questionable from a moral point of view, it is nevertheless a form of being which with its questionable aspects belongs to the basic images of living reality and therefore, in the Greek view, demands reverence, if not for all of its various expressions still for the totality of its meaning and being."

Should once such a "basic image of living reality" as this Hermes-world be elucidated, it would not merely be held together and characterized by its specific logic, it would also become lucid and convincing even to us. On the other hand, this capacity for illumination creates a distance from the more primitive and less intelligible image of Hermes which is shown to us in most of the Priapic statues, in the ithyphallic stones (the "Herms"), not to mention the Titanic and ghostly aspects of this Deity. Otherwise one *can,* in fact, speak of Hermes as a "way of being" who is at the same time an "idea," and on these grounds proclaim deep truths about the God. His way is — to cite once more the classical description by Otto — "so unique and so fully delineated, it moves so unerringly through all his activities, that one has only to notice it once to have no further doubt as to his essence. In this we recognize both the unity of his activities and the meaning of his image. Whatever he may do or produce reveals the same idea, and that is Hermes."

The correctness of these words is as convincing as was that of the previous quotations. And yet we must ask: does this rigid adherence to an idea that is still plausible to us, to a way of being in the world that we can still experience, and by which we would, like the Greeks, adjudge divinity, not exclude from the outset an important part of the Hermes image and of the Hermes-world? Would this not exclude precisely something "Greek"

4

that historically and significantly belongs to Hermes? Granted, this would be a meaning that must disclose itself to us as something both new and age-old, and also as something reaching beyond our historical vision, and perhaps even beyond our philosophical convictions. For if we are to have success in reviving the God's image in its fullness, we must be prepared not only for what is immediately intelligible, but also for what is strangely uncanny. Indeed, the images of the Greek Gods can be so resistent to conceptualization and logic that one can be tempted in the course of an investigation to quote the famous lines that were spoken to describe human beings:

> I am not a cleverly worked-out book,
> I am a *God* with his self-contradiction... *

2 *The Hermes of the* Iliad

Let us first become familiar with what can be learned about Hermes from the Homeric poems. It would certainly be a rash conclusion to maintain that those features of the Hermes image which are not mentioned in the *Iliad* or in the *Odyssey* or in the Homeric Hymn were unknown to the author of that particular work. For every missing feature that makes

---

*These two lines, in which the word "God" has been exchanged for "Man," are from Conrad Ferdinand Meyer's "Huttens letzte Tage."

an appearance in one of the other sources and is sufficiently ancient we must ask what the reason for this silence might have been. That we learn more about Hermes in the *Odyssey* than in the *Iliad,* and more in the Hymn than in the *Odyssey,* has a very obvious reason: the heroic world of the *Iliad* is much less the world of Hermes than is that of the journey epic, the *Odyssey,* and his world becomes more apparent still in the Hymn, not because the Hymn originates later than the two great epics, but because it has the God himself for its hero.

The world of the *Iliad* is not the world of Hermes. If there is one figure who dominates this world and gives it a characteristic stamp, it is Achilles, just as Odysseus dominates and characterizes the world of the *Odyssey.* The world of the *Iliad* receives its essential tone from the finality of the fate that befalls its short-lived hero. To the view that life is once-and-for-all and inwardly destined corresponds the view that death is equally final and obedient to the same law — an unalterable, conclusive end. The hero's daimon of fate, which comes into being with him at his birth — his own personal *Ker*[2] — ripens into a daimon of death, and the soul, which is the suffering aspect of the same daimon, complains loudly against its fate, for it leaves behind manhood and youth for a bloodless and shadowy existence in death. No escape from this is possible. Life is individual: it actualizes itself according to the inherent laws which govern the particular hero in question, and it ends in his own particular death. The hero is not tricked or seduced by an unfamiliar death-daimon. The power that lures him to his death is originally in him — in Patroclos, in Achilles, in Hector, in all who through their heroic courage fall to it. Not

6

once in the *Iliad* does Hermes appear to lead a soul away or to assume the role of escort.

The reason is obvious: Hermes' sphere of activity lies outside of this world in which death forms the adamantine background as the concluding and excluding polar opposite of life, which the hero chooses at the same time as he chooses his heroic existence. That Hermes is not the guide of souls in the *Iliad* does not necessarily mean that he is not the guide of souls in general, but only perhaps that in the world of Hermes death itself has a different appearance. What we do discover in the *Iliad* about the world and activity of Hermes refers to alternatives of life, to the dissolution of fatal opposites, to clandestine violations of boundaries and laws. Death can be viewed from life's point of view as its destined conclusion and necessary dissolution through its opposite. Life's most obvious alternative course — its overflowing in generation and productivity, in fruitfulness and multiplication — appears, however, as something incalculable, as purest accident. At just this point in the *Iliad* we meet Hermes.

It is Hermes whom his beloved Phorbas thanks for a wealth of herds (Book XIV, 490). Hermes, too, was the lover of Polymele, daughter of Phylas, whom he visited secretly in her home and who bore him a son, Eudoros (Book XIV, 180ff.). With such references the warm air of procreation and enriching fruitfulness wafts into the atmosphere of the *Iliad*, which is otherwise so heavy with dire fatefulness. (The names Phorbas, Polymele and Eudoros even suggest wealth of herds and freely-given abundance.) Hermes is deliberately kept at a distance from every heroic happening. Not that he is totally devoid of every trace of fatality. The language of the epic often

7

names him Argeiphontes, instead of Hermes. It is a name meant to recall a Titanic feat: slaying the many-eyed Argos with a sickle-sword, the same sword Kronos used to maim the sky God and Perseus used to severe the head of the Medusa.[3] The constant epithet for Argeiphontes, *diaktoros*, ("guide"), is related to words that refer to the dead ones and to the wealth that falls to them.[4] His characterization as *akakēta* ("benignant," "gracious") witnesses to a gentle death-God. The best translation of this epithet is "the painless one." Not even in the battle of the Gods, lacking in tragedy as it is, does Hermes take part.[5] A Goddess, significantly, not a God, is assigned to be his opponent — Leto, the Mother-Goddess who closely resembles her daughter, Artemis. But Hermes is too clever to engage in combat with her,

> since it is a hard thing
> to come to blows with the brides of Zeus
> who gathers the clouds. No,
> sooner you may freely speak among the
> immortal gods, and claim that you were
> stronger than I, and beat me.
>
> (Book XXI, 498-501)

With these words he evades Leto. Fame has absolutely no part in his world. Hermes' skill in the *Iliad* is strictly that of the most unheroic evasion. The office of messenger of the Gods, which he otherwise occupies, he does not hold in the *Iliad*; any allusion to this is avoided.[6] He has his place among the other Gods, qualified by his own mastery: he is the master thief. He stole Ares, who was bound up in chains, out of his prison (Book V, 390), and he should also have stolen the corpse of Hector had only the Gods been in agreement (Book XXIV, 24ff.). Zeus prefers what he considers a better expedient, though he still works through Hermes. The entire final bitter-sweet book, in which the heroic world of the *Iliad* suddenly displays its unpredictable tenderness, stands under the sign of Hermes. Zeus sends him to the aged Priam, who is just then on the way to retrieve from Achilles the body of his son. He is sent not as a messenger – the messenger of Zeus in the *Iliad* is Iris – but as a guide (*pompos*). For it is Hermes who likes to associate with a person ("Hermes, for to you beyond all other gods it is dearest to be man's companion ..." Book XXIV, 334-35), to grant a request, and to make a person invisible. This is what he does here, first ingratiating himself with the old man in the form of a youth and then leading him in the ways of the thief. With his help it is possible to steal the corpse away from the unrelenting demon of revenge that possesses Achilles and the entire Greek camp. Achilles obeys Zeus and gives in, but it is left to Hermes to open the way for escape, and he does so by putting the guards to sleep.

This youthfully handsome, friendly, and thievish guide, who possesses magical golden shoes which transport him over earth and sea and a magical staff with which he puts people to sleep and awakens them again – has he not all the characteristics and attributes of a seductive and lethal guide of souls, the gentle psychopomp of the later monuments? The reason the poet does not allow him to appear in this role is, as we have seen, because it would not conform to the world of the *Iliad*. The world of the *Odyssey* confirms this opinion, and it also allows this aspect of Hermes to come to the fore.

3   The Hermes of the Odyssey

The last book of the *Odyssey* begins with an epiphany of Hermes:

> Meanwhile the suitors' ghosts were called away
> by Hermes of Kyllene, bearing the golden wand
> with which he charms the eyes of men or wakens
> whom he wills.
>
> He waved them on, all squeaking
> as bats will in a cavern's underworld,
> all flitting, flitting criss-cross in the dark
> if one falls and the rock-hung chain is broken.
> So with faint cries the shades trailed after
> Hermes, pure Deliverer.
>
> He led them down dank ways, over grey
> Ocean tides, the Snowy Rock past shores
> of Dream and narrows of the sunset,
> in swift flight to where the Dead inhabit
> wastes of asphodel at the world's end.

The death of the suitors was not a sad-though-harmonious conclusion to an heroic existence; their gluttonous lives were extinguished with unexpected suddenness by the avenging arm of the returning husband. Almost like animals they were slaughtered, their lives left unfinished (as measured against the standard of the hero) by this sudden death, cut down just as they were in the midst of their youth. They fell like dull animals, mere carcasses, as though the souls in their bodies had been choked off. Then

10

Hermes "summoned" their souls. This word "summon" (*exekaleito*) would otherwise be translated "to conjure up," as one does spirits of the dead who sojourn in the grave or in the underworld. Here, however, Hermes shows himself as the summoner of souls *before* burial, not for the purpose of forcefully calling the souls back, but to beckon them away gently to the distant meadows on the other side. The staff which he holds in his hand discloses its connection to a kind of "lulling to sleep" (*ommata thelgein*) and "re-awakening" that is different from what occurs in the last book of the *Iliad* where these words appear in their original meaning. There it is really only a matter of sleeping and awakening; here the text speaks of death, but of death not as an unambiguous and final event. Re-awakening in this context also contains a double meaning: it can refer to an escape from death itself.

The staff that has these qualities is beautiful and golden. It establishes a distance between the God and the dark swarm of bat-souls. To be sure, this staff can also appear as horribly upsetting if, like Horace, one considers it from the viewpoint of the one being led away:

> His grisly wand let Hermes once uphold,
> The blood returns not to the formless shade
> The sable company he troops below
> In idle ears against their doom appeal.
> (*Odes*, Book I, XXIV.)

But when the poet celebrates the God, he emphasizes the golden color of the "grisly wand":

11

Thou layest unspotted souls to rest;
Thy golden rod pale spectres know;
Blest power! by all thy brethren blest,
Above, below.

(*Odes,* Book I, X.)

Here there is mention of the fortunate souls which even in the underworld
will not be completely deprived of light. In Homer, the gleam of tangible
sunlight belongs exclusively to the God. Homer depicts the guide of souls
in his divine substantiality, as distinguished from the insubstantial swarms
that plunge into the other world. Gentle, his golden staff gleaming, Hermes
appears even among the musty paths of ghosts. Here, too, he is named
akakēta, "painless," since he does no harm even to these unfortunate
souls. On the contrary, his presence softens the effects of Odysseus' fear-
ful revenge, just as the ferocity of Achilles was calmed in the last book of
the *Iliad,* which, as we saw, stands under the influence of Hermes. The
great difference in this case is that he reveals his gentle, golden aspect in a
world which is not restricted to only "this side," but rather in a world whose
hero and symbol is Odysseus.

The *Odyssey* is not a poem of heroic life that is set off starkly against a
background of once-and-for-all, irrevocable death; it is rather the poem of
a kind of life that is permeated with death, in which death is continuously
and incessantly present. The two poles — life and death — fuse here. The
world of the *Odyssey* is an existence in flux that is continuously in contact
with death, as warp with woof. It consists as much of its background and
underground, of the yawning abysses beneath and behind, as it does of itself. Odysseus continuously moves over and through these. But not only

12

is *his* existence in the *Odyssey* characterized by this movement; Telemachos, too, hovers between life and death, as do, also, the suitors. Particularly caught in this suspension is the one who waits, Penelope. But in the most proper and strictest sense, the one who is suspended over the gulfs and chasms of existence is Odysseus.[7]

We previously called the *Odyssey* a journey epic, and we must now imagine the often experienced reality of "journeying" as something very special, in contradistinction to "roaming" or "traveling". Odysseus is not a "traveller." He is a "journeyer" (even if this is sometimes *malgré lui* — "in spite of himself"), not simply because of his moving from place to place, but because of his existential situation. The traveller, despite his motion, adheres to a solid base, albeit one that is not narrowly circumscribed. With each step, he takes possession of another piece of the earth. This taking possession is, of course, only psychological. In that with each extension of the horizon he also expands himself, his claim of possession on the earth expands continuously as well. But he remains always bound to a solid earth beneath his feet, and he even looks for human fellowship. At every hearth that he encounters he lays claim to a kind of native citizenship for himself. For the Greeks, the approaching stranger is *kat' exochēn* ("an outstanding eminence") and *hiketēs* ("one who comes to seek protection," "a suppliant" or "fugitive"). His guardian is not Hermes, but Zeus, the God of the widest horizon and the firmest ground. In contrast, the situation of the journeyer is defined by movement, fluctuation. To someone more deeply rooted, even to the traveler, he appears to be always in flight. In reality, he makes himself vanish ("volatizes himself") to everyone, also to himself. Everything around him becomes to him ghostly and improbable, and even his own reality appears to him as ghostlike. He is completely absorbed by movement, but never by a human community that would tie him down. His companions are the companions of the journey: not those he wants to lead home, as Odysseus his comrades, but those he joins, as it is said of Hermes in the *Iliad* (Book XXIV, 334-35). With companions of the journey, one experiences openness to the extent of purest nakedness, as though he who is on the journey had left behind every stitch of clothing or covering. Do not today those who wish to be free of the bonds to the community in which they grew up and to which they were intimately bound, who want to be open to each other without reservation or boundary, as two naked souls — do they not go on a wedding journey (*Hochzeitsreise*)? Is this journey not a *"Heimführung"* ("taking home" the bride) as well as an *"Entführung"* ("elopement"), and therefore also "hermetic"? Journeying is the best condition for loving. The gorges over which the "volatized one" passes like a ghost can be the abysses of unbelievable love affairs — Circe and Calypso islands and holes; they can be abysses also in the sense that there no chance exists for standing on firm ground, but only for further floating between life and death.

The journeyer is at home while underway, at home on the road itself, the road being understood not as a connection between two definite points on the earth's surface, but as a particular world. It is the ancient world of the path, also of the "wet paths" (the *hygra keleutha*) of the sea, which are above all, the genuine roads of the earth. For, unlike the Roman highways which cut unmercifully straight through the countryside, they run snakelike, shaped like irrationally waved lines, conforming to the contours of the land, winding, yet leading everywhere. Being open to everywhere is part of their nature. Nevertheless, they form a world in its own right, a middle-domain, where a person in that volatized condition has access to everything. He who moves about familiarly in this world-of-the-road has Hermes for his God, for it is here that the most salient aspect of Hermes' world is portrayed. Hermes is constantly underway: he is *enodios* ("by the road") and *hodios* ("belonging to a journey"), and one encounters him on every path. He is constantly in motion: even as he sits, one recognizes the dynamic impulse to move on, as someone has acutely observed of his Herculean bronze statue.[8] His role as leader and guide is often cited and celebrated, and, at least since the time of the *Odyssey*, he is also called *angelos* ("messenger"), the messenger of the Gods.

We would have to devote special attention to the office of the divine messenger if we wanted to exhaust its whole meaning. As just an intimation of this we will mention that Hecate, too, as well as Hermes, may transport souls (both being guardians of the underworld), and she is also an *angelos*. Iris, too, has a connection to this Goddess, which is established by the presence of her cult on the Hecate island near Delos. To the essence of Iris, however, belongs the unreachable distance of a celestial sign, such as the rainbow, whose name she bears. Thus she fits into the world of the *Iliad* as a messenger of the Gods. "Tidings" (*"Angelia"*) – a daughter of Hermes according to Pindar – descends from the Gods more frequently when the boundaries between life and death, time and eternity, earth and Olympus are open. And they open easily when they are as volatized as they are in the world of the *Odyssey*. We find that the Gods sent Hermes to Aigisthos with a warning, though it was in vain (Book I, 38). And we see him hurrying to Calypso with the command of Zeus:

15

No words were lost on Hermes the Wayfinder,
who bent to tie his beautiful sandals on,
ambrosial, golden, that carry him over water
or over endless land in a swish of the wind,
and took the wand with which he charms asleep —
or when he wills, awakens — the eyes of men.
So wand in hand he paced into the air,
shot from Pieria down, down to sea level,
and veered to skim the swell. A gull patrolling
between the wave crests of the desolate sea
will dip to catch a fish, and douse his wings;
no higher above the whitecaps Hermes flew
until the distant island lay ahead.....

(Book V, 37-49)

Just as it needs no further explanation here that Hermes is the divine messenger, and needs none when he appears in the last book as guide of souls, so it needs none when he appears in an other characteristic place of the *Odyssey,* on the island of Circe, as the wise-to-magic savior of the hero. He meets Odysseus so naturally there that Odysseus shows no surprise when Hermes gives him his hand, addresses him, and offers him the antidote to the magic potion of Circe (Book V, 277ff.). Just where the atmosphere of the *Odyssey* is most thickly clouded with spooky possibilities, there the presence of Hermes is least surprising. And Odysseus himself, who drifts about within this atmosphere, has a wholly personal relation to Hermes. On his mother's side he descends from Hermés, although not much is made of this in the *Odyssey*; more is said of his grandfather, Autolycos, who was also mentioned in the *Iliad* as the arch-thief of the heroic age. Autolycos was a son of Hermes, who, like his father, was a master in the art of taking oaths (*Iliad,* Book XIX, 395). He honoured Hermes especially (19, 397). Odysseus says to the faithful swineherd, Eumaios, that all people owe it to this God (Hermes) if their works are blessed with "grace and fame" (*charis kai kudos*) (*Odyssey*, Book XV, 320), even those who are servants. There can be no doubt that the gift of cunning belongs to the Hermes-Autolycos line, only in Odysseus it no longer possesses the primordial mythic dimensions that it had for them. Odysseus is merely "*polytropos*" ("versatile"), while Autolycos, according to one source, possessed the capacity to transform himself, and, according to another source, he made invisible everything he touched.[9] The "art of oath-taking," in its primordial mythic dimensions, is described for us in the Hymn to Hermes.

4   *The Hermes of the Hymn*

The poet of the Hymn to Hermes presents primordial mythological material in a form that could later be integrated into and become part of the classical tradition. The serenely scintillating, waggish irony with which he glorifies the Titanic event corresponds also to the attitude of his hero. What additional information we get here about Hermes does not so much enlarge his portrait to include new aspects as deepen it towards the Titanic. Since he is integrated into the world of Zeus, Hermes naturally does not belong to the race of Titans. Yet as we follow him we sense in him the essence

17

of the pre-Olympian world, even apart from the fact that he appears as a divine child and that the childhood of the Gods belongs not to Olympian myth but to a far more ancient mythology.[10] In the Hymn, an Olympian God grows out of the primal child, and with this development his pre-Olympian history becomes included in his classical image. We should really study the whole poem in detail, but we hope to do an adequate job of understanding it by interpreting only key passages.

> Of Hermes sing, O Muse, the son of Zeus and Maia,
> Lord of Kyllene, and Arcadia rich in sheep, the
> fortune-bearing Herald of the Gods ...[11]

Two associations to Hermes, who is being celebrated here, are emphasized straight away. The one is to a Greek province where he was especially honored, Arcadia, and in particularly to a mountain there which was the location of his cult, Kyllene. To these is associated the myth of his birth, which in itself as a primal child mythologem antedates the Olympian order, yet is easily spliced into that order. The other association is to the Olympians: Hermes belongs to them as their messenger. For this role he receives the Homeric epithet *eriounios*, often incorrectly translated "the beneficial one." A comparison with an Arcadian gloss[12] reveals a meaning that could very well belong also to a death God: "the quick one." In fact, there is one case in which two chthonic Gods who receive human sacrifices are named *eriounioi*,[13] and Aristophanes declares outright that the *Eriounios Hermēs* is the *chthonios*. The basic meaning revealed here – "fast as death" – suits the messenger Hermes, not only as an Arcadian or Kyllenian Diety but also as an Olympian. These two poles – the provincial cult and the Olympian

18

office — define him not as one who flucutuates, but as one who is coming into existence. What sort of coming into existence is the birth of a God? A Greek poet imagined it:

> him who Maya bore, the fair-tressed majestic
> nymph, that lay in the arms of Zeus: a shamefaced
> nymph was she, shunning the assembly of the
> blessed Gods, dwelling within a shadowy cave.
> Therein was Cronion want to embrace the fair-
> tressed nymph in the deep of the night, when
> sweet sleep held white-armed Hera, the immortal
> Gods knowing it not, nor mortal men.

In comparison to the Goddesses who are at home on the bright heights of Olympus, Hermes' mother is a mere nymph. She is a Goddess who is bound up with the Arcadian landscape, originally probably a type of primordial mother-daughter Goddess.[14] Her name is sometimes Maia (which as an appellative is a designation of old women: the grandmothers and wet-nurses), sometimes *Maias*, that is, "daughter of Maia." Her associations with the audacious Titan Atlas, whom Hesiod names as her father, and with the sky as the eldest of the Pleiades, suggest a Titaness. In the Hymn she receives the epithet *aidoiē* ("majestic"), which in Hesiod is applied to the primal Gods of the Titan period, the *theōn genos aidoion* ("the respected race of Gods"). She did not escape from the "sacred congregation of the Gods," as some translations have it, but rather she "shunned" it (*ēleuato*) and took up abode in a cave (*antron naiousa*). There she and Zeus begat Hermes. Stolen love, but for that reason all the more fully enjoyed (*misgesketo*),[15] deepest night (*nuktos amolgōi*), sleep as a helper in deceiving

19

Hera (as he [*Dios apatē*] helps deceive Zeus in the *Iliad*), and above all secrecy (*lēthōn*) — these elements are woven together to formulate the first phase in the evolution of Hermes. In this not only is a "wish" of Zeus fulfilled, as the German translation states, but through this fulfillment his *noos* ("mind" or "insight") achieves its end (*Dios noos exeteleito*). The second stage in the evolution of Hermes is this:

> But when the mind of great Zeus was
> fulfilled, and over her the tenth moon
> stood in the sky, the babe was born to
> light, and all was made manifest.

This coming into being, this birth, is revelatory: *eis te phoōs agagen, arisēma te erga tetukto* ("it came to light, and all the works were revealed"). The revelation comes by stages. First, the newly born God himself becomes manifest through the association — or, one could say, in the constellation — of various elements. This God is Hermes, with characteristic Hermetic attributes:

> Then she bore a child of many a wile and
> cunning council, a robber, a driver of the
> kine, a captain of raiders, a watcher of
> the night, a thief of the gates ...

Let us examine these attributes. "The painless one" is missing; nowhere in the whole Hymn does the epithet *akakēta* appear. Hermes is here merely the "ruler of dreams" (*hēgētōr oneirōn*), not the "leader of souls". To this we could perhaps compare the Homeric passage in which the dream-like people of Phaiakia — a Hermetic people,[16] worthy of the world of the

Odyssey – sacrifice to Hermes before going to sleep (*Odyssey*, Book VII, 138); yet the last book of the *Odyssey*, with the epiphany of the psychopomp, is again removed into the distance of another world. Missing here, too, is any hint of Phaiakian mildness; we must think rather of the deceitfulness of misleading dreams. All the rest of the attributes testify to this. The first of these, *polytropos* ("wiley"), is the well-known epithet for Odysseus. And *pylēdokos* ("gate-watcher") in the last line would not mean "guard of the gate", but rather the dangerous "nocturnal scout" (*nuktos opōpētēra*) who takes his unsuspecting victim on the dark street at the city gate. We are faced with the skilled highwayman and bandit, as well as the flattering deceiver.

We are prepared, then, for the second phase of Hermes' revelation, "who soon should show forth deeds renowned among the deathless Gods." There follow now as further revelations the deeds which the poet combines with the first stage (the birth) into a temporal sequence of three, and he ties this trinity to the number four, which is also temporally conceived:

> Born in the dawn, by midday well he harped,
> and in the evening stole the cattle of Apollo
> the Far-darter, on that fourth day of the
> month wherein lady Maia bore him.

The association of Hermes to the number four certainly does not originate with our poet: it is at least as ancient as the Hymn and probably much older. The birthdays of the Gods were not established in the cults without some rationale. The fourth day of the month was, for example, sacred not only to Hermes but also to Aphrodite,[17] who is closely connected to him

21

in other ways as well. The solid association of Hermes with the number
four is further testified to by the fact that in Argos the fourth month had
the name Hermaios.[18] The quaternity was for the ancients one of the most
constant constituents of the Hermes image; they further acknowledge this
in the four-cornered form of the Herms. The late author, Murtianus Cap-
pella, summarizes the general opinion: *numerus quadratus ipsi Cyllenio depu-
tatur, quod quadratus deus solus habeatur* ("the quadratic number is reck-
oned to Cyllenius itself, because it is possessed by the quadratic God alone").
Whether the quadratic image or the birthday on the fourth day of the month
came first is unimportant. We are dealing here with a basic number, an expression of divine totality, which the poet playfully links with the trinity.
The number three also is not alien to Hermes: he is shown with three heads,[19]
and his staff in the Hymn is "golden and three-pointed." In this poetic
play the birth coincided with the morning, and the pure harmony of the
lyre at noon is not accidental. For Pindar the sunbeams themselves are the
hammers that play this divine instrument, whose tones create order just as
does the light of the sun. We need not take special pains to point out that
the darkest aspect of Hermes appears with the coming of night. In all of
this the process of revelation is linked in the simplest and most natural way
with the brightening and darkening face of the cosmos. But is the revelation to be seen as primarily an interpretation of this natural cycle? As we
stand with the poet on the day of Hermes' birth, the "first of Tetras," are
we merely confronting the natural world? Or are we participating in a
leap of imagination that creates the world of Hermes, that re-arranges the
natural world into the special cosmos of Hermes, that gives the world the
face of Hermes? The answer to this admits of no doubt. The revelation

proceeds by leaps and bounds outward from within itself:

> Who, when he leaped from the immortal
> knees of his mother, lay not long in the
> sacred cradle, but sped forth to seek the
> cattle of Apollo, crossing the threshold
> of the high-roofed cave.

The text speaks literally of a leap (*hog' anaixas*). With this begins the rushing advance of Hermes, which moves at once to a further revelation of his essence:

> There he found a tortoise, and won endless
> delight, for lo, it was Hermes that first
> made of the tortoise a minstral. The
> creature met him at the outer door, as
> she fed on the rich grass in front of the
> dwelling, waddling along ...

Meeting and finding are revelations of Hermes' essence. That the poet is fully conscious of this is indicated by the words he associates with the find: *murios olbos* ("endless delight"). With this he has entered explicitly into the sphere of Hermes: "happiness and riches" are, according to line 524, products of Hermes' staff. "*Olbos,*" which is here even "endless," means fortune, but, more than that, it tends toward implying solid and true happiness. Hermes' relation to happiness and fortune, which is recognized by the whole tradition, begins now to show its particular feature. According to the *Iliad* he bestows fortune through fruitfulness and this belongs (as was already pointed out) to the wider field of accidental happenings. In the *Odyssey* he, along with the other Gods, is called "giver of excellent gifts"

23

(Book VIII, 335, 325). Only now in the Hymn does the Hermetic gain reveal its finding and thieving features.

Accidental discovery is in itself not yet quite Hermetic; it is merely the stuff of Hermetic activity, which is then shaped to the meaning of the God. In every cosmos the accident remains fundamental, a residue of the chaotic primordial condition,[20] and this is true also of the Hermetic cosmos. Hermes has taken control of his cosmos, and through him every find, which in itself belongs to the Gods and not to man, becomes a theft that is put to better use. The Greek word for windfall, *hermaion*, signifies that it belongs to Hermes. This was also the name given to the offerings that were left at the roadside Herms. These were windfalls for hungry travelers who stole them from the God — in his own spirit, just as he would have done. According to antique understanding, the general meaning of Hermes proceeded from this pilfering at the Herm.[21] Hermes sanctions the act if the accidental find is seized as a theft, whether or not it falls immediately in his realm. Correspondingly, the robber takes his booty just as Hermes would have done — as a find. Should two people set out on an undertaking together, they call to one another "*Koinos Hermēs*," which means "a theft done together" rather than " a find made together"; better yet, it means "a find and a theft done together." Fundamentally this is the motto of every business undertaking. Even the most honest business is directed toward a no-man's land, a Hermetic intermediate realm that exists between the rigid boundaries of "mine and yours," where finding and thieving are still possible. Mere unscrupulousness, however, is not of itself Hermetic; with it belongs intelligence and the art of living. Should a stupid fellow have good luck, he owes it to the witless Hercules, who was especially honored as a God of luck in Italy. Such a person becomes *dives amico Hercule* ("rich friend of Hercules"). The precious little mythologem to which Horace alludes (Sat. II, 6, 10ff.) is told by his interpreter Porphyrio. Mercurius once let Hercules talk him into enriching a stupid man. Mercurius showed him a treasure which he could use to buy the piece of land he was working. He did so, but then proved himself unworthy of the Hermetic windfall by continuing to work the same piece of land!

We come now to the place in the Hymn where an accidental discovery — a mythological primal animal, the tortoise[22] — becomes an Hermetic work of art:

> ...at sight whereof the luck-bringing son
> of Zeus laughed, and straightway spoke, saying:
> "Lo, a lucky omen for me, not by me to be
> mocked! Hail, darling and dancer, friend of
> the feast, welcome art thou! Whence gatst thou
> thy gay garment, a speckled shell, thou, a
> mountain-dwelling tortoise? Nay, I will
> carry thee within, and a boon shalt thou be
> to me, not by me to be scorned, nay, thou
> shalt first serve my turn. Best it is to
> bide at home, since danger is abroad. Living
> shalt thou be a spell against ill witchery,
> and dead, then a right sweet music-maker."
> So spoke he, and raising in both hands the
> tortoise, went back within the dwelling,
> bearing the glad treasure. Then he choked
> the creature, and with a gouge of grey iron

he scooped out the marrow of the hill
tortoise.

Here it is not "the luck-bringing son of Zeus" who laughs, speaks, and
acts, but rather the "swift as death son of Zeus" (*Dios eriounios huios*).
The irony of his words springs from his divinity and is as merciless as Being
itself. It is based on "seeing through." Seeing through is divine. Greek tragedy offers its spectators a divine standpoint in that it allows them to par-
ticipate in such a penetrating vision. The spectator sees in the king the
guilty fugitive while he is still ruling and governing. In the same way Hermes "sees through" the tortoise. There is no doubt what he sees there. He
names the unsociable beast with an expression that alludes to a divinely established designation of the lyre, "friend of the feast."[23] He sees already
the glorious instrument while the poor tortoise is still alive. For the tortoise,
that glory means a painful death. If the "through-seer" of such a fate is God,
he makes light of the irony of the situation that is visible only to him. But
it is Titanically cruel-hearted if he bursts out laughing at what he sees,[24] if
his words make that irony dazzlingly manifest, and if his violent deed helps
to fulfill that destiny. This is what Hermes does, not naively, but roguishly
and without compassion. The cruelty of his irony reaches its height in his
roguish use of the proverbial line: "Best it is to bide at home, since danger
is abroad." On the other hand, the divine scoundrel does have a point, for
out of his victim's death he conjures music, this unique way for mortal humans to transform the harshness of existence into Phaiakian mildness.
"Cheerfulness and love and sweet slumber" are, according to Apollo, the
gifts of this Hermetic art, which Hermes translates into a revelation of his
essence. Originally, music was the gift of Hermes, and in the tones of the

26

syrinx it remains so. This is not Apollonic music. Let us listen to the song
that Hermes sings to the first notes of the lyre:

> Then took he his treasure, when he had
> fashioned it, and touched the strings in
> turn with the *plectrum*, and wondrously it
> sounded under his hand, and fair sang the
> God to the notes, improvising his chant
> as he played, like lads exchanging taunts
> at festivals.

The song of Hermes is no less roguish than were his words: it is compared to the impudent mocking songs that Greek youths would fling back
and forth at one another. If his words previously were cruelly ironic, they
now show him to be utterly without shame. It is possible that a verse following the first line has been lost;[25] nevertheless the translation remains
certain in all essentials. Hermes sings of two themes: love and riches. The
second of these corresponds to an aspect of him that we have already discussed. The first theme reveals a side of him that until now has been hidden,
the one that knows no shame.

> Of Zeus Cronides and fair-sandalled
> Maia he sang how they had lived in
> loving dalliance, and he told out the
> tale of his begetting, and sang the
> handmaids and the goodly halls of the
> Nymph, and the tripods in the house, and
> the store of cauldrons.

Hermes sings insolently of the love affair of his parents. One should not

27

think that this was customary among the Greeks. The Homeric style, which in general is also characteristic of the Hymn, is very restrained in erotic matters. At the same time, however, it is not at all prudish. It is simply stated when and where a love union took place, if this is in any way important, but the full details are never given. The single exception is the song of the Phaiakian minstrel, Demodokos, which tells of the surprised lovers, Aphrodite and Ares. This song conforms to the atmosphere of the Phaiakians, which within the Hermetic world of the *Odyssey* corresponds to the gentlest aspect of Hermes. In that song, too, the shamelessness of Hermes is revealed for the first time in the classical tradition. In Demodokos' song he appears with the other Gods who have been called together by the cockold Hephaistos as witnesses to his own shame, to view the glorious pair caught in the net. Asked by his brother Apollo if he would like to share the couch with the Goddess even though thus bound up in chains, Hermes, to the hearty laughter of the other Olympians, shows his colors with these words:

> "Would I not, though, Apollo of distances!
> Wrap me in chains three times the weight of these,
> come goddesses and gods to see the fun;
> only let me be bestride the pale-golden one!"
> (Book VIII, 339-42)

That finding and thieving in the realm of love are also Hermetic traits needs no further comment:[26] a secret love affair was the first stage in the evolution of the God. It was, in relation to Hera, thievish love; in relation to Zeus and the nymph, it was a love affair ("*Liebeshandel*") in what is perhaps the full meaning of this ambiguous word. The original text speaks explicitly of "Hetaira love" (*hetaireiē philotēs*). This can also be unselfish love that is snatched in the spirit of Hermes. And it would be shameless in the Hermetic sense to ask if there might not after all be some connection between this love relationship and the treasures of Maia, who, according to Hermes' words (11. 167ff.), has no connection to riches.

The Hermetic traits, which the Hymn now reveals in the motifs of finding and thieving, seem to be almost entirely negative: the negative aspects of the ithyphallic Herms, the shamelessness. This shamelessness reaches its apex in the song about the love affair of his own parents. In all this negativity, however, something very precise and very positive is expressed. Without question, the Herm expresses the essentially phallic nature of the God, but just what this "essentially phallic" nature may be has yet to be answered by the Hymn. The Hymn's mode of expression is every bit as restrained as that of the Homeric epic. On the other hand, how far it is from any sort of prudishness is shown in the scene (11. 293-98) where the little rogue behaves toward Apollo in a truly indecent way. In the present passage he speaks of the *oaridzein* ("to hold bold converse with") of Zeus and Maia in "*hetaireiē philotēs*" ("hetairic love"). The first word refers to the talk of lovers and is later applied to the merry-making of the Gods on Olympus (1. 170). It is, however, a phallic word, although as finely literary as "*Minne*"; in the same sense, the entire Hymn to Hermes may be called a highly literary monument to phallic shamelessness.

We must observe, however, that there is a kind of reticence in the Hymn: the explicitness of the Herms is not matched in the tone or contents of the Hymn. Why not? Not because of prudishness or literary restraint. The

29

first is simply not present, and the indecency of line 296 defeats the second. The real reason is yet to be discovered. For now, we may realize what the Hymn specifies as the core and the meaning of the shameless song. A further statement is added to the line telling of the love of Zeus andMaia: "and he told the tale of his begetting ..." In this translation *geneē* is rendered as "begetting"; it is important, however, to understand the meaning of this word more exactly. The basic meaning of concrete "kinship" or "family" is not indicated here, but rather the abstract "origin," which in the heroic period was just as real as the other. For Hermes this is additionally important because of his position on Olympus. His impudent song is a *genealogia*; as such it completes the mythology, and even substitutes for it. Mythology deals with origin(s) as basic reason for everything that exists in the present or will exist in the future. In the genealogy, ancestors of "famous names" (*geneēn onomakluton*) occupy the place of origin, as emergence proceeds forth from the primordial depths. The genealogy turns the great original mythic theme into a family tree.[27] The family tree must begin, of course, with the earliest Gods. This is the manner of Hesiod's *Theogony*. Another way is that of the Hymn, in which Hermes "names his praiseworthy descent." His impudence proves to be the conscious return of the offspring to his source. Indeed, Hermes' impudence is the consciousness of his own origin and reason for being, an unbroken and linear consciousness of his development which is — as the development of the God has shown us — a further characteristic feature of Hermes.

The clue to understanding this consciousness more exactly comes to light in the second song that Hermes sings, with which he enchants Apollo.

We will look at it now, even though it occurs much later in the Hymn:

> He sang the renown of the deathless Gods,
> and the dark Earth, how all things were
> at the first, and how each God got his
> portion.

> To Mnemosyne first of Gods he gave the
> meed of minstrelsy, to the Mother of the
> Muses, for the Muse came upon the Son of
> Maia.

> Then all the rest of the Immortals, in
> order of rank and birth, did he honour, the
> splendid Son of Zeus, telling duly all the
> tale, as he struck the lyre on his arm.

Hermes here presents a full-blown theogony. Hesiod begins with praise to the Muses. It is natural that a God should begin further back toward the source, with the mother of the Muses. The Great Goddess Mnemosyne, one of the wives of Zeus, may be compared to a source (*Quelle*) for several reasons. (It is not meaningless that she has a spring – *Quelle* – in Lebadeia; it is also significant that her daughters are figures analogous to the spring Goddesses.[27a]). She is memory as the cosmic ground of self-recalling which, like an eternal spring, never ceases flowing. She even grants, again precisely through the Muses, pleasant, healing lapses of memory (*Theogony* 55); in these one does not forget oneself, but only what is meant to be forgotten. For this reason the blessings of Mnemosyne aid the dead and the poets: the first she does not allow to dry up, the second she causes to flow over. In the Hymn she appears as the Goddess who is set over Hermes like a dai-

31

mon of fate. This is the meaning of the original text: *hē gar lache Maia-dos huion* ("For he was ordained the son of Maia"). It is the fate of Hermes that for himself and for those with him there is no chance of losing oneself. He cannot ever escape from memory. He is possessed by it, and he carries it as inherited knowledge of all primordial sources of being. In this his consciousness reveals itself more exactly as spiritual-psychological, just where we believed we would be able to recognize its phallic aspect.

We need not give up either of these two understandings of Hermes. The Titanic element, to which the phallic aspect can belong,[27b] breaks furiously to the fore the moment he ceases to play the lyre for the first time:

> So then he sang, but dreamed of other
> deeds; then bore he the hollow lyre and
> laid it in the sacred cradle; then, in
> longing for flesh of kine, he sped from
> the fragrant hall to a place of outlook,
> with such design in his heart as reiving
> men pursue in the dark of night.

In the divine singer — in the shameless, Titanic one — the thief was already present. An inordinate hunger for meat awoke in him: *kreiōn eratidzon* ("being extremely greedy for meat") is the phrase in the text, which in the *Iliad* is applied to a lion. As the story unfolds it becomes clear that this hunger brings something un-Olympian and Titanic to light. Instead of devouring the two animals which he separates from the others and slaughters, he sacrifices them to the twelve Gods in a way that is both exemplary and skillful (Odysseus as beggar has this skill and owes it to Hermes). The bloody offering is a Titanic practice, invented in its simple form by Prometheus, who, in accordance with his Titanic nature, tries to get the meat for himself.[27c] Hermes shows his Olympianism by counting himself as one of the twelve Gods (through his birth their number becomes even and complete) and, like the distant heavenly ones, by taking part in the offering only symbolically and not giving way to his greed for meat.

> Anon, glad Hermes dragged the fat portion
> on a smooth ledge, and cut twelve messes
> sorted out by lot, to each its due meed he
> gave. Then a longing for the rite of sacrifice
> came on renowned Hermes: for the sweet savor
> irked him, immortal as he was, but not even
> so did his strong heart yield ... The fat
> and flesh he placed in the high-roofed stall,
> the rest he swiftly raised aloft, a trophy
> of his reiving.

The entire theft must be seen from the beginning in the light of this accentuated divine standpoint. It is not the Titanic prank of a divine wonder-child told merely for the sake of entertainment; it is revelation of divine essence and fundamentality. His thieving is the *neē phōrē*:[28] not "childish theft," but "new theft" or "new larceny," the Hermetic theft, which is only now being introduced into the world. Earlier there existed thieving only through use of power and might, Titanic thieving. Hermes states explicitly — we will hear it later in the Hymn — that he could also plunder Apollo's treasures at Delphi. He consciously refrains from indulging in a Titanic power-play, which would be less than divine. He possesses the power, the slyness, the lack of scrupulosity for it. What holds him back is his divine nature, through which the Titanic nature changes into ingenious charm

33

and loses its violence. Hermes reveals a new kind of thieving or larceny, a divine kind. Apollo suffers no loss from it; indeed he gains the lyre and a singularly related, yet antagonistic, brother. Instead of violence there appears here inventiveness and animated swiftness. Everything moves ahead by leaps and bounds (*alto* — "nimble," 65; *theōn* — "running," 70), as does Hermes' revelation itself from the moment of his birth, and as do his actions in the remainder of the Hymn (*sumenōs* — "running, darting," 150; *anorouse thoōs spoudēi iōn* — "he leaped up quickly and made haste," 415; *essumenōs* — "hastily," 320; *speudonte* — "he hastened," 397; *errōsanto* — "they moved rapidly," 505). All of this is befitting to this God (as it is to Apollo also[29]). As a babe he does not yet have his wingled sandals, so he invents them out of tamarisk and myrtle branches, not only to confuse the pursuer with the prodigious tracks, but also to make use of the speed given by the myrtle, a plant with an explicit connection to death.[30] In this way he drives the cattle and yet avoids the rigors of traveling (*hodoi-poriēn aleeinōn* —"avoiding the journey"). According to the *Odyssey* the magic powers of plants are familiar to him, and he works magic also with the branches that Apollo wants to use to bind him (1. 140). In every sense his art is enchanting. The master enchanter volatizes himself before our very eyes like a breath of wind. Returning home from his novel thievery,

> Hermes, son of Zeus, bearer of boon,
> bowed his head, and entered the hall through
> the hole of the bolt, like mist on the
> breath of autumn. Then, standing erect, he
> sped to the rich inmost chamber of the cave,
> lightly treading noiseless on the floor.
> Quickly to his cradle came glorious Hermes

and wrapped the swaddling bands about his
shoulders, like a witless babe, playing
with the wrapper about his knees. So lay
he, guarding his dear lyre at his left
hand. But his Goddess mother the God did
not deceive; she spake, saying:

"Wherefore, thou cunning one, and whence
comest thou in the night, thou clad in
shamelessness? Anon, methinks, thou wilt
go forth at Apollo's hands with bonds about
thy sides that may not be broken, sooner
than be a robber in glens. Go to, wretch,
the Father begat thee for a trouble to
deathless Gods and mortal men."

But Hermes answered her with words of
guile: "Mother mine, why wouldst thou scare
me so, as though I were a redeless child,
with little craft in his heart, a trembling
babe that dreads his mother's chidings?
Nay, but I will essay the wiliest craft to
feed thee and me for ever. We twain are not
to endure to abide here, of all the deathless
Gods alone unapproached with sacrifice and
prayer, as thou commandest. Better it is
eternally to be conversant with Immortals,
richly, nobly, well seen in wealth of grain,
than to be homekeepers in a darkling cave.
And for honor, I too will have my dues of
sacrifice, even as Apollo. Even if my father
give it me not I will endeavour, for I am of
avail, to be a captain of reivers. And if

35

the son of renowned Leto make inquest for
me, methinks some worse thing will befall him.
For to Pytho I will go, to break into his
great house, whence I shall sack goodly
tripods and cauldrons enough, and gold, and
gleaming iron, and much raiment. Thyself,
if thou hast a mind, shalt see it."

So held they converse one with another,
the son of Zeus of the Aegis, and Lady Maia.

The arrival of Apollo gives Hermes the chance to show his skills once
again:

Now when the son of Zeus and Maia beheld
Apollo thus in wrath for his kine, he sank
down within his fragrant swaddling bands, being
covered as piled embers of burnt tree-roots are
covered by thick ashes, so Hermes coiled himself
up, when he saw the Far-darter; and curled
himself, feet, head, and hands, into small
space (summoning sweet sleep), though of a
verity wide awake, and his tortoise-shell
he kept beneath his armpit. But the son of
Zeus and Leto marked them well, the lovely
mountain nymph and her dear son, a little
babe, all wrapped in cunning
wiles. Gazing round all the chamber of the
vasty dwelling, Apollo opened three aumbries
with shining key; full were they of nectar
and glad ambrosia, and much gold and silver
lay within, and much raiment of the Nymph,
purple and glistering, such as are within the

36

dwellings of the mighty Gods. Anon, when he
had searched out the chambers of the great hall,
the son of Leto spake to renowned Hermes:

"Child, in the cradle lying, tell me
straightway of my kine: or speedily between us
twain will be unseemly strife. For I will seize
thee and cast thee into murky Tartarus, into
the darkness of doom where none is of avail.
Nor shall thy father or mother redeem thee
to the light: nay, under earth shalt thou
roam, a reiver among folk fordone."

The "folk fordone" — this phrase trying to convey the meaning of *oligoi
andres* in the original — are most likely the dead, who drift about insub-
stantially with a "frail buzzing" or "chirping" (*tetriguiai*); they are the
"likenesses of living creatures" as the *Odyssey* expresses it. Here, for the
first time in the Hymn, this connection between Hermes and the dead is alluded to. Apollo threatens him with confinement in that dark underground
realm, where he can spend his time leading the souls around. For a moment
the image of psychopomp emerges, thus making way for the sly psychagoge,
for the shameless guide of souls, for the prototype of all future rhetoricians
and sophists, for Hermes Logios. In the following speech the "art of oath-
taking," too, is practiced in the words of the original sophist:

Then Hermes answered with words of
craft: "Apollo, what ungentle word hast thou
spoken? And is it thy cattle of the homestead thou comest here to seek? I saw them
not, heard not of them, gave ear to no word
of them: of them I can tell no tidings, nor

37

win the fee of him who tells. Not like a
lifter of cattle, a stalwart man, am I: no
task is this of mine: hitherto I have other
cares: sleep, and mother's milk, and about
my shoulders swaddling bands, and warmed
baths. Let none know whence this feud arose!
And verily great marvel among the Immortals
it would be, that a new-born child should cross
the threshold after kine of the homestead; a
silly rede of thine. Yesterday was I born,
my feet are tender, and rough is the earth
below. But if thou wilt I shall swear the
great oath by my father's head, that neither
I myself am to blame, nor have I seen any other
thief of thy kine: be kine what they may, for
I know but by hearsay."

So spake he with twinkling eyes, and twisted
brows, glancing hither and thither, with long-
drawn whistling breath, hearing Apollo's word
as a vain thing. Then lightly laughing
spake Apollo the Far-darter:

"Oh, thou rogue, thou crafty one; verily
methinks that many a time thou wilt break
into stablished homes, and by night leave
many a man bare, silently pilling through
his house, such is thy speech today! And
many herdsmen of the steadings wilt thou
vex in the mountain glens, when in lust for
flesh thou comest on the herds and sheep thick
of fleece. Nay come, lest thou sleep the
last and longest slumber, come forth from

> thy cradle, thou companion of black night!
> For surely this honour hereafter thou shalt
> have among the Immortals, to be called for
> ever the captain of reivers."
>
> So spake Phoebus Apollo, and lifted the
> child, but even then strong Argus-bane had
> his device, and, in the hands of the God,
> let forth an Omen, an evil belly-tenant, with
> tidings of worse, and a speedy sneeze there-
> after. Apollo heard, and dropped renowned
> Hermes on the ground.

This final indecency places Hermes at the opposite pole from the mor-
tally clean God Apollo;[30a] yet, at the same time, through his lyre he remains
extremely close to him. It is incomparable how this infant is able to show
us the whole breadth and range of the Hermetic world. We think of Horace,
the poet of indecent Epodes and of light, delicate, dignified Odes, for whom
Mercurius was the protector and divine model.[30b] He names him beloved in all
spheres: *superis deorum gratus et imis* ("Pleasing thus the gods of the up-
per regions / And of the lower") (*Odes* I, 10). After this all that is left in
the Hymn is that the value of this extensive realm, in which even the lowest
is not unholy, be recognized on Olympus, and that harmony be brought to
the border-line between the fraternal (but conflict-laden) spheres of Hermes
and Apollo.

The recognition of Hermes comes in Zeus' outburst of laughter, when
the new-born infant dares to repeat his artful perjury in the presence of his
father (368ff.). Apollo, too, laughed at the first oath of the thief. This is

that divine laughter that vouches for the harmlessness of the Titanic heritage of the Gods within their own circle.[31] In the reciprocal delineation of spheres, Apollo receives the lyre and Hermes the cattle and symbol of shepherdhood, which in this case is not a shepherd's staff, but a whip (497). This attribute is distinguished by its form from the splendidly rich staff of Hermes, which is called "golden" and "triple-leafed." Whether this is a description of the caduceus, the staff of the herald, which appears so frequently on monuments, remains very questionable. For the time being, Hermes has only the form of a herald (331). We will soon see in what connection the Hymn mentions his ambassadorial office; the caduceus with its double serpent motif may very well originate in that sphere. Here it seems much more that Apollo is simply turning over to his brother all relations that he previously has had to a specific aspect of the chthonic world, to his possessions of herds and other treasures.[32]

Of great significance is the dividing up of the oracle. Apollo retains for himself what "lies in the mind of Zeus alone" (535), his "secret counsel" (538). Only he can use it to help human beings, or to punish them if they earn such treatment through their probing curiosity. He does not trust Hermes with such an exalted calling; indeed, he addresses him in this important passage not as an equal, but as the "Eriunios Daimon of the Gods" (551). "Daimon," if not exactly disparaging, lies less near the detached divinity of an Apollo and closer to a meeting with and touching of the mortal. The great revealer of truth does, however, leave to the swift-as-death daimon a peculiar oracle. It is in the form of the three "praiseworthy sisters," whose names are not given. The description of them is a puzzle, which is inten-

40

tional since this is suited to oracular language (553):

> there be certain Thriae, sisters born, three
> maidens rejoicing in swift wings. Their
> heads are sprinkled with white barley flour,
> and they dwell beneath a glade of Parnassus,
> apart they dwell, teachers of soothsaying.
> This art I learned while yet a boy I tended
> the kine, and my Father heeded not. Thence
> they flit continually hither and thither,
> feeding on honeycombs and bringing all
> things to fulfillment. They, when they are
> full of the spirit of soothsaying, having
> eaten of the wan honey, delight to speak
> forth the truth. But if they be bereft of
> the sweet food divine, then lie they all
> confusedly.

They are bees — this is the solution of the riddle. For the ancients, bees have a maidenly quality. Moreover, bees "rejoice in swift wings," as the text states. Their "heads" come up covered with pollen, as if "sprinkled with barley flour." They feed on "honeycombs," or more precisely they feed on the wax with which they will build their honeycombs. They satisfy themselves with honey. They swarm about gifted children and lend them the gifts of the muses.[33] They also have souls; indeed, for antiquity they are pure souls.[34] Bees that are sated with the "sweet food of the Gods" — honey[35] — are like souls full of enthusiasm. The word for their "swarming about" (*thuiōsin*) means the swarming of the furious Maenads. These enigmatic sisters are bees, but as bees they are souls, whose ability or inability to prophesy depends on whether they are "full" or "empty". The Hermetic oracle is dependent on these conditions, conditions which we find expressed in pure intellectual form in Plato's *Symposium*.

The later classical tradition knows nothing of this anymore. Hermes' connections to dice and lotteries and other oracles of chance are familiar.[36] Less frequently one finds Hermes as the general master of animals, since Apollo extends to his brother the power over herds (567ff.). At the end Apollo says something significant about Hermes' messenger role:

> "And let him alone be herald appointed
> to Hades, who, though he be giftless,
> will give him highest gift of honour."

What kind of a "herald" Hermes would be for the house of Hades is indicated in the second clause: for this ambassadorial office he receives nothing (*adotos per eōn*). For who rewards a herald who performs such a task? "Not the worst gift" (*geras ouk elachiston*) is how the mysteries express their view of death. Doubtless the psychopomp and his office are meant here. He is a "herald appointed to Hades," and this is on the strength of his ordination. This is clearly signified in the first clause: *oion d'eis Aidēn tetelesmenon angelon einai* ("and let him alone be herald appointed to Hades"). The word *tetelesmenon* means a bit more than merely "proper" or "correct" (as it is translated into German; the English translation omits it. *Tr.*). Preceding the *tetelesmenon einai* there must unconditionally be a *telein* ("to carry out a transaction"), a formal preparation and appointment. This "making ready" is in Greek linguistic use an ordination, even if it be so only in a figurative sense. One could be "initiated" or "ordained" into the position of commander of troops; the word would then relate to the outcome of an election. According to our text, therefore, Hermes became messenger and escort to Hades only after a preliminary ceremony had been completed. To think of an ordination is justified by the whole context. It belonged to the essence of the Greek mysteries that through their initiations one came into friendly relation to Hades. (From this it follows that for one who is initiated, death is "not the worst gift.") About the ordination of the feminine *angelos*, Hecate, we have the report that she received her initiation from the Kabeiroi. Only after this is she supposed to have been connected to Hades.[37] Hermes has the closest possible relation to the Kabeirean mysteries. It seems that one is led here beyond classical tradition to an at least equally ancient mystical tradition.

We are now at the end of the Hymn:

> With such love, in all kindness, did
> Apollo pledge the son of Maia, and thereto
> Cronion added grace. With all mortals and
> immortals he consorts. Somewhat doth he
> bless, but ever through the dark night
> he beguiles the tribes of mortal men.

The deceptions of Hermes are harmless only for the Gods. Like everything else Titanic, these deceptions dissolve in the laughter of the Olympians. For humans it turns out differently, especially if they meet up with the arts of Hermes in his special element, the night. In the night he executed his first theft. Indeed, for his sake the moon rose twice and thereby doubled the night. Apollo called him a "companion of black night" (290). After the theft "he lay dark as night in his cradle" (358), and deepest night belonged to the constellation of his conception and coming into being. It

43

is certainly significant that the Hymn, which has celebrated him in birth as
the "watcher of the night" in the sense of a dangerous adventurer, closes
with this dark aspect of the God.

5 *Hermes and the Night*

The basic texts of the classical tradition have been open before us. We
do not need to introduce those later texts that merely preserve this tradition or vary it slightly. An example of this is a tale that appears in a Hymn
to Hermes by Alkaios: the little cattle thief steals also the bow and quiver
from his threatening brother.[38] Whether he appears as child, youth, or
adult, we confront in Hermes a surprising image. We see his earnest bearded
face against a white-grounded sepulchral vase from a period of high attic art;
he is holding out his hand to someone who is already no-one. We see in another of these wonderful representations how the dead woman loses herself
in the depths of the eyes of the seductive guide of souls. In appearance he
may have become more detached and even more sublime than he was, for
example, on that archaic vase-painting where, sickle-sword in hand, he is
hastening away to slay the Argos, or on another which shows him winged,
sitting with his magic wand, a conjurer of the spirits of the dead. We can
set up around ourselves a whole gallery, including those spiritualized epiphanies on the attic grave *lekythoi*. If through the vase-painting of the fifth

century we reach a fourth, psychic dimension, we still really only get closer to those fields of asphodels that make up the volatizing, devouring back-ground of the mild, but relentless and unyielding psychopomp: he himself, however, has not become any less mysterious.

We are not merely trying to establish the identity of a name, but rather to apprehend always the same God. For the Greeks he was what is depicted in the classical tradition, which includes also the pictorial representations. In his "such-ness," he is an historical fact which cannot, by strict and honest historical means, be reduced to something else: neither to a concept, to a "power," nor to a "spirit" — a gravestone or signpost spirit[39] — not even to an idea that would not contain in a nutshell everything that Hermes' "such-ness"constitutes. What Otto's brilliant description of Hermes allowed of the God to shine forth proved itself correct and in accordance with the interpretations of the texts, but it was not the "totality" of him, which is really the "truth." Incorrect was the negative part of the statement. "In the new religion — as the Homeric-classical period is called there — Hermes is not a God of procreation and fertility, even if he can appear as such, since his wonderful rule also leads toward the good of love's union and generation of children. It is always the magical escort that determines the content of his activity, the leading to a precious gain ..." "The procreative power is positively not the essence of Hermes."

The correct, positive statement — that the world of Hermes stands under a "special sign, namely that of deft guidance and sudden gain" — does not, however, exhaust that world. To that world belongs also the rejected parts and the disavowed: the phallic as well as the spiritual, the shameless as well

as the gentle and merciful, even if the connection between all these qualities does not seem to make sense. As a reduction of the Hermes world, the
sentence, "In the favor of the Guide is revealed the true essence of the God,"
is not much better than its reduction to a hypostasis of a general divine
readiness to help and a devilish joy at others' misfortune, all in one person.

What are we trying to say when we conceive the "such-ness" of Hermes,
as historically presented in texts and on monuments, as a Hermes world?
The multiplicity of the tradition suggests this term. "World" can be a comprehensive idea if as an autonomous entirety it accommodates the observer
as if he were moving about in the world he normally is surrounded by. The
world of the *Iliad* or that of the *Odyssey* accommodates us in this way.
Every such world, however, is at the same time a worked-out idea of the
world that existed already prior to this expression of it and that lent itself
to the finished expression of the idea. There can be no "world" — even if
it is the purely spiritual epiphany of an intellectually luminous God — which
is not "worldly," that is, which does not function as a space to contain the
content of the revelation in a fitting way. If a God is "idea" and "world,"
he remains nonetheless in connection with the world that contains all such
"worlds"; he can be only an "aspect of the world," while the world of
which he is an aspect possesses such idea-aspects. Indeed, it has the ability
to shine forth in its totality as idea, it possesses the light of the idea and is
itself in its own way lighted and clear.

There are words in which this notion appears as the ancient, long since
forgotten wisdom of languages: the Hungarian *világ* means "light" and
"world," and the derivative adjective *világos* ("light" and "clear") can also

46

mean "world-like." "Light" and "clear" in the sense of "world-like" – and therefore convincing – could also be the idea of Hermes. Indeed, only then would it be a "basic form of living reality." It would be such a basic form for another reason, namely that it, like reality always does, contains so much that is obscure for us. What has been passed down by tradition would really make up a realistic "world," which as idea would perhaps gradually dawn even on those of us who are accustomed to philosophical and not to mythological ideas.

The forerunner of the modern concept of the antique Gods as ideas, Goethe's friend Karl Philipp Moritz, has the sentence in his *Handbook of the Gods* (*Götterlehre, oder mythologische Dichtung der Alten,* 3rd ed., Berlin, 1804),[39a] just where he is treating Mercury, that "to a certain extent, and when looked at from a certain exalted standpoint, every divine form comprehends within itself the essence of all things." The author of the classical description of Hermes, Walter F. Otto, is unwillingly a true disciple of Moritz, in that he conciously adopts an exalted standpoint, and looking from there perceives in the Greek forms of divinity the "essence of things," namely, the meaning of a realm of being whose living spirit – but a spirit made of the same material, a kind of spiritual condensation – appears as the respective Godhead. However elevated this point of view may be, it must seek its justification in the realistic worldliness of the divine images as apprehended from this perspective. So, for Otto, Hermes is on the one hand "the spirit of a configuration of existence which returns again and again under the most dissimilar conditions"; on the other hand, he is the spirit of a completely concrete "world-like" aspect of the world that ac-

47

commodates us always again in a special realm — he is "a spirit of night."
The question is whether the "world-likeness," which is offered through the
association to night, really does completely fill the image of Hermes as it is
handed down and make it convincing, even while, perhaps, remaining par-
tially obscure.

Nyx, the Goddess of Night, is at any rate not identical with Hermes, and
Apollo distinguishes his brother from her sufficiently when he calls him "fellow of the night." Yet, as Otto correctly points out, we automatically think
of Hermes in connection with much that the Greeks said of Night. This is
not part of the classical tradition, but concerns something that corresponds
to it. Let us read the superbly beautiful pages which Otto, in his portrait
of Hermes, devotes to the experience of night.

> A man who is awake in the open field at night
> or who wanders over silent paths experiences
> the world differently than by day. Nighness
> vanishes, and with it distance; everything
> is equally far and near, close by us and yet
> mysteriously remote. Space loses its measures.
> There are whispers and sounds, and we do not
> know where or what they are. Our feelings, too,
> are peculiarly ambiguous. There is a strangeness
> about what is intimate and dear, and a seductive
> charm about the frightening. There is no longer
> a distinction between the lifeless and the living,
> everything is animate and soulless, vigilant and
> asleep at once. What the day brings on and makes
> recognizable gradually, emerges out of the dark
> with no intermediary stages. The encounter

suddenly confronts us, as if by a miracle:
What is the thing we suddenly see — an
enchanted bride, a monster, or merely a log?
Everything teases the traveler, puts on a
familiar face and the next moment is utterly
strange, suddenly terrifies with awful
gestures and immediately resumes a familiar
and harmless posture.

Danger lurks everywhere. Out of the dark
jaws of the night which gape beside the
traveler, any moment a robber may emerge
without warning, or some eerie terror, or the
uneasy ghost of a dead man — who knows what may
once have happened at that very spot? Perhaps
mischievous apparitions of the fog seek to
entice him from the right path into the desert
where horror dwells, where wanton witches dance
their rounds which no man ever leaves alive.
Who can protect him, guide him aright, give
him good counsel? The spirit of Night itself,
the genius of its kindliness, its enchantment,
its resourcefulness, and its profound wisdom.
She is indeed the mother of all mystery. The
weary she wraps in slumber, delivers from care,
and she causes dreams to play about their souls.
Her protection is enjoyed by the unhappy and
persecuted as well as by the cunning, whom
her ambivalent shadows offer a thousand
devices and contrivances. With her veil she
also shields lovers, and her darkness keeps
ward over all caresses, all charms hidden and

revealed. Music is the true language of her mystery — the enchanting voice which sounds for eyes that are closed and in which heaven and earth, the near and the far, man and nature, present and past, appear to make themselves understood.

But the darkness of night which so sweetly invites to slumber also bestows new vigilance and illumination upon the spirit. It makes it more perceptive, more acute, more enterprising. Knowledge flares up, or descends like a shooting star — rare, precious, even magical knowledge.

And so night, which can terrify the solitary man and lead him astray, can also be his friend, his helper, his counselor.[40]

Having entered with Otto into his experience, we may well ask: is not then Night the very stuff of Hermes? that which gives him reality? Yes, if one knows the God beforehand and brings his image along, then one recognizes in him the familiar characteristics of the night and vice versa. Yet, one does not find *all* the Hermetic characteristics in Night. Something essential is missing. Otto himself admits as much, even though he takes this telling point rather lightly. "This picture," he continues after his description of the night experience, "falls short of a true likeness of Hermes, but it does have something of all of his charateristics. We need only transpose it to a more masculine and saucier pitch and the spirit of what is peculiarly Hermes will stand before us."[41] But precisely this more masculine and audacious aspect, this active essence, would have to be removed from the Hermes idea if we wished to discover its worldliness in the connection to night. The passivity of night and the active quality of the traditional Hermes separate these two aspects of the world at their very cores.

But is the world of active and audacious masculinity, which befits Hermes, a less nocturnal world than that of night itself? Is not this active world present in those parts of the human and animal worlds of which Hermes has been given charge? — and where the act of becoming takes place? In this Hermes-world there is naturally also entropy: this is the night in another sense, in an Hermetic sense, the night of the psychopomp. The night of generation and the night of dying, do we not carry these in us? — an undivided night, which is happy to join itself to the night "out there," as a twin sister of the great, all-inclusive world?

From simply the "night out there" one could not derive the robber or the thief, not the psychopomp nor the impudent God of the Hymn to Hermes. From the poet of the Hymn we learned about his birth and development. We know where he comes from and what type of consciousness he exemplifies. He is most likely the same dark depth of being from which we all originate. Perhaps for this reason Hermes can so convincingly hover before us, lead us on our ways, show us golden treasures in everyone through the split-second timing which is the spirit of finding and thieving — all of this because he creates his reality out of us, or more properly through us, just as one fetches water not so much out of a well as through the well from the much deeper regions of the earth.

We turn now to the monuments and documents of antiquity, which show

51

Hermes in the closest relation to the origins of life and to immortality. His world revealed itself in classical tradition as one that is more directed outward. Despite the thievery and deceit and shamelessness — and this is probably the most wonderful thing about it — a divine innocence is properly suited to and inherent in it. Hermes has nothing to do with sins and atonement.[42] What he brings with him from the springs of creation is precisely the "innocence of becoming."

PART TWO

THE HERMES OF LIFE AND DEATH

1 Hermes and Eros

The answer to the question, "What appeared to the Greeks as Hermes? " can, on the basis of the classical tradition, be expressed as follows: he is the supra-individual source of a particular world-experience and world-configuration. Certainly there is also an experience of the world that rests on the basic assumption that a man stands in the world alone, endowed only with a consciousness that is exclusively restricted to the ability of receiving scientifically evaluated sense impressions. No such assumption exists, however, when it comes to that other experience of the world which the antique statements correlate with Hermes. The experience of the world in this manner is open to the possibility of a transcendent guide and leader who is also able to provide impressions to consciousness, but of a different kind: impressions that are palpable and manifest, that in no way contradict the observations and conclusions of natural science, and yet extend beyond the attitude described above, which is the common one today. With Hermes as leader in life — so the classical tradition teaches us — the world receives a special nuance, the Hermetic accent as we have become acquainted with it. This Hermetic aspect is thoroughly empirical, and it remains within the realm of a natural experience of the world. The sum total of pathways as Hermes' playground; the accidental "falling into your lap" as the Hermetic material; its transformation through finding — thieving — the Hermetic event — into an Hermetic work of art, which is also always something of a tricky optical illusion, into wealth, love, poetry, and every sort of evasion from the restrictions and confinement imposed by laws, circumstances, destinies — how could these be *merely* psychic realities? They are *the* world and they are *one* world, namely, that world which Hermes opens to us.

The reality of the Hermes world proves at least the presence of a standpoint from which it is revealed; more than that, it testifies to something active that is not merely revealing itself from that standpoint, but that is ever again suddenly present and drives the world to give concrete expression to the Hermetic works of art and illusion. The source of this experience and configuration of the world, which at the mention of Hermes' name breaks into the light of day (and broke forth also without mentioning his name, only less clearly), is Hermes himself. It must possess the complete Hermetic breadth, from the phallic to ... From here we are as yet unable to move on with any perspicacity, for on the basis of the classical tradition we have to complete the foregoing sentence with: ... to the guidance of souls, an activity that stretches even beyond life. Here Hermes remained completely enigmatic to us. We experienced the world with him in the Hymn to Hermes. If we did not know it beforehand, we must have discovered there that

one has a different experience of the world with an antique God than one
would have without him. Speaking mythologically, each God is the source
of a world that without him remains invisible, but with him reveals itself in
its own light, and this world passes beyond the world-picture of natural
science. Hermes too, therefore, is more than merely the luminous idea of
a world. He is its source, through whom that world originated and through
whom it becomes intelligible. As the basis of understanding the world, he is
also idea, though one we have not yet fully grasped. The nocturnal God of
adventurers seems to stand alone in Greek mythology, without parallel and
altogether strange.

"On the day of Aphrodite's birth," begins a well-known mythologem,

> the gods were making merry, and among them
> was Metis's son Resource [Poros], the son of Craft. And
> when they had supped, Need [Penia] came begging
> at the door because there was good cheer inside.
> Now, it happened that Resource, having drunk
> deeply of the heavenly nectar — for this was
> before the days of wine — wandered out into
> the garden of Zeus and sank into a heavy
> sleep, and Need, thinking that to get a child
> by Resource would mitigate her penury, lay
> down beside him and in time was brought to bed
> of Love [Eros]...
> As the son of Resource and Need, it has been
> his fate to be always needy; nor is he delicate
> and lovely as most of us believe, but harsh and
> arid, barefoot and homeless, sleeping on the
> naked earth, in doorways, or in the very streets

> beneath the stars of heaven, and always partaking
> of his mother's poverty. But, secondly, he brings
> his father's resourcefulness to his designs upon
> the beautiful and good, for he is gallant, impetuous,
> and energetic, a mighty hunter, and a master of
> device and artifice — at once desirous and full of
> wisdom, a lifelong seeker after truth, an adept
> in sorcery, enchantment, and seduction.[1]

The mythologem later speaks of those conditions of fullness and emptiness that according to the Hymn apply also to the Hermetic oracle. Those bees are related to this Daimon, Eros. "In the space of a day," it is said of him,

> he will be now, when all goes well with him,
> alive and blooming, and now dying, to be born
> again by virtue of his father's nature, while
> what he gains will always ebb away as fast.
> So Eros is never altogether in or out of need ...

It is not necessary to point out that we are dealing here with the great Daimon of Plato's *Symposium*. The myth is told by Socrates, who is supposed to have heard it from the wise priestess of the Arcadian Mantineia, Diotima. This source reference is certainly not without basis and meaning.[1a] To what extent this mythologem is based not only on Plato's vision but also on an older religious tradition one will never know exactly. Moreover, such a differentiation is of no importance for our purposes. Plato's genius here brings forth a genuine mythologem. The method of characterizing a divine being by means of his becoming is the same here as in the Hymn to Hermes. Here as there, these are realities, which are being apprehended mythologically.

The relationship among these realities – Poros and Eros to Hermes – is what concerns us.

If Eros is a reality – and for Plato he is, as he is for anyone who has experienced him – then Poros, who has the positive qualities of Eros, is even more so. As in Hesiod's geneology of the Gods, the more content a figure has and the more he encompasses the cosmos and contains the world (or, to use our earlier term, the more world-like[2] he is), the higher he stands. This is the case with Poros. He is not an invention of Plato's, used to provide Eros with an abstraction for a father. Alkman, a lyrical poet of the seventh century, mentions him with Aisa as one of the two oldest dieties (*geraitatoi siôn*), against whom no amount of heroism can prevail (Fr. 1, 13ff.). The antique interpreter makes the additional remark that Poros is here identical with Hesiod's Chaos. Yet, while this oldest being of the *Theogony* is original formlessness, lacking direction or movement and taking back into itself everything that has form, Poros, according to his name and his son, seems to be the world's fullness on its path towards free unfolding in eternal movement forward, masculine and active, prepared for ambush and attack and overflowing with every kind of creativity and fruitfulness. Aisa, who is paired with him as the feminine principle, can only signify the restriction and limitation that is tailored to the fate of the individual. The unrestricted movement of Poros is indicated also in this, that heroism, when compared to him, is named *apedilos* – "without winged sandals." "No man may fly to heaven," warns the next passage.

Similar to this father is Eros, the Hermes-like God of adventurers. How does Eros, then compare to Hermes himself? In many ways he shares with him the Hermetic range of being. On the one hand, he is a divine child who had a very ancient cultic monument in Thespiai — a crude stone, compared to which the phallic Herms show much greater differentiation.[3] On the other hand, Hesiod, the poet from Askra, which is not far from Thespiai, describes him much as does the great love poem. In the *Theogony* he appears with Gaia, immediately after Chaos, as the third Being and brings with him activity and movement, the driving force that unfolds in progeny, something which that masculine or feminine primal Being does not possess.

Most likely, therefore, he is the first masculine Being in the cosmos, but he is also, as he "unfolds his limbs," "spiritual" or "psychic," as are Fainting and Death. And he is no less swift than swift-as-death Hermes. He comes soaring on his wings, if not literally so in Hesiod, just so, according to the primitive mythological account, in the Orphic cosmogony.[4] Wherein the negative aspects show themselves already for Hesiod lies in this: "he overpowers the insight in the breast and the rational counsel of all Gods and men" (*Theog. 122*). This limitation through Eros occurs all the more with the profusion of the erotic. According to Plato he brings wonderful memory, the luminous understanding of the spirit, but not the cold calculating cleverness of Hermes. Though far removed from blind compulsion,[5] Eros does not however signify the Hermetic freedom of soaring flight for which he gives wings to even the most sluggish souls. Even the spiritual part of Eros, the memory of determinative primordial images, flows into bonds and ties. Predestination, regulation by primordial images, idealism belong to Eros. For this reason the love poems written in his spirit are so completely different from those of Horace, which came into being under the sign of Her-

mes.[6] Looked at from the world of Hermetic possibilities, Eros, despite
his comprehensive nature, appears limited — a somewhat more idealistic and
less cleverly turned-out, dumber son of Hermes.

For us it is at least a hint toward understanding the Hermes idea that the
nature of Eros includes phallus, soul, and spirit, and that he even reaches out
beyond the life of the individual. For this reason, traditions in which Eros
is in fact a son of Hermes hold a special importance for us. They do not belong to the classical tradition but form another alongside it, one that is more
shrouded in mystery. Cicero, who preserves this tradition for us in his works
on the Gods (*De natura deorum* III, 23, 60), recalls in one passage the "wri-
ters of more secret texts," *qui interiores scrutantur et reconditas literas.*
There he shares the results of such research in a systematically organized,
formal way. The different variations of myths are simply listed with a dis-
tinction made between various Gods of the same name. According to this
system, the first Eros was a son of Hermes and the first Artemis, the second
Eros was the son of Hermes and the second Aphrodite: *Cupido primus Mercurio et Diana prima natus dicitur, secundus Mercurio et Venere secunda.*

The question of a mystical tradition, to which the ending of the Hymn
to Hermes alludes, still remains open. Still unexplained, too, was the reticence of the Hymn, which we noticed in contrast to the explicitness of the
ithyphallic Herms. These are yet unresolved problems, and behind them
beckons still the enticing mystery of Hermes. We will now go on to consider less classical phenomena, present them and let them speak for themselves, as the classical tradition spoke for itself.

59

2 Hermes and the Goddesses

Hermes as the companion of Goddesses is well-known also in the classical tradition. In the *Odyssey* Eumaios, who lives out in the woods, offers a portion of the slaughtered swine to the nymphs and to Hermes (Book XIV, 435); in this he bears witness to a long-standing, ancient connection among these Dieties. The Homeric Hymn to Aphrodite speaks of this in more detail (11. 257ff.). The nymphs, who in the *Odyssey* are mentioned *before* Hermes, are according to their portrayal there neither immortal Goddesses nor human women. With them trees came into being, and along with their long-lived mistress they finally pass away. In the classical conception, not even the nymphs of wells and springs live forever.[7] For this reason they are all the more generous with their gifts. They are the wet-nurses for divine and semi-divine children. They enjoy the "immortal foods of the Gods" and perform beautiful round dances with them. According to a later passage in the Hymn to Aphrodite, it is these nymphs "with whom the Silenoi and the excellent scout, the Argos-slayer, make love in the depths of the lovely grottos." Hermes appears here for the first time in a list with the Silenoi, those half-animal and (above all) phallic creatures. But whereas the Silenoi seem to be there merely as the masculine counterpart and completion of the feminine nature-spirits, Hermes, in this relationship to the nymphs, is less one for whom the nymphs embody the Eternal-Feminine which he has to serve than one for whom they are the opportunity that he eternally masters.

Yet, this is only one aspect of this relationship. For in the cult of the nymphs, as we know it particularly from countless votive reliefs in the hills and caves of Attica, Hermes is expressly assigned to the Goddesses as their

permanent escort (*synopaōn*). On the reliefs he is always leading a threesome of them, the smallest choir so to speak, just as he was also coordinated
with the three Charities on the Acropolis in Athens.[8] As though he were un-
veiling a mystery, he leads the earnestly striding threesome up to us, to tell
us that it is just these three who allow everything to burst into life in the
deeps of the caves, the springs, the roots, the hills. On a wonderful marble
tablet stands a worshiper, who is depicted as much smaller than the others
and who is being shown this "holy revealed mystery" of untamed fruitfulness, its feminine nature to which however also belongs a masculine compo-
nent.[9] As much as the classical conception may distribute the feminine aspect of the world among springs and streams, grottos and trees, with this
threesome it is certainly hinting at the primordial image of that Great Goddess, of whom we know that she is a trinity.[10] If primal femininity was
assigned to a tree as its nymph, so that both would have to die when the
tree was felled, Great Demeter, too, the most maternal of the feminine trin-
ities, would also feel its pain. The connection between the Great Goddess
and a nymph is neither obvious nor classical either. It is expressed by the
Hellenistic poet Kallimachos in the language of feeling (Hymn. 6, 40). It existed, as the holy groves of Demeter or Persephone demonstrate, alongside
the classical tradition. The revelation of the Feminine as three distinct figures means only that the original core-knowledge of one Great Goddess with
three aspects has been dissolved in classical imagery. In that original understanding, the triad was still one: a maidenly being, maidenly not like human
brides but like springs and all primal waters, who became a primal mother
and then re-appeared once again in her bride-like, maidenly daughter. The
more secret traditions illuminate the relationship of Hermes to this primor-

61

dial feminine being.

Cicero, basing himself on a lost mythologem, [11] reports that Hermes is supposed to have fathered Eros with the first Artemis. According to another myth, the second Aphrodite became through Hermes the mother of a second Eros. Both of these stories, as well as other reports of Hermes' love affairs with Great Goddesses, can be combined into a genuinely pre-Olympian mythological story. Here, unlike the account in the Kyllenic birth mythologem that we know from the Hymn, Hermes is not made into a son of Zeus and integrated thereby into the Olympian world order. He is a son of Ouranos and Hemera, "Heaven" and "Bright Day," and he becomes priapically aroused through catching sight of a Goddess. [12] Although this scene is supposed to have been played out in northern Greece (we will soon learn about the scenery), this mythologem could well be the text for the ithyphallic representations of Hermes, which show him as the phallus. [13] This mythologem can hardly be understood as merely an invention that was intended to explain the cultic monuments. What it relates is a primordial mythological theme of the greatest significance: it is the first evocation of the purely masculine principle through the feminine.

Do we know for sure, then, that the primordial mythological Hermes, of whom we are now speaking, was an unequivocally masculine being before this scene was enacted? The opposite is much more likely to have been the case. Aphrodite, the daughter of Ouranos and Hemera, is called his sister; for her, too, this parentage is meaningful. Her descent from the sky-God is confirmed by another birth account in the primal-mythological style, in Hesiod. [14] Her luster matches the light-nature of Hemera, while Hermes'

62

nocturnal nature does so to a much lesser extent. The androgenous first being, who since Theophrastus has been known as Hermaphroditos and as such has been ascribed to Hermes and Aphrodite as their son, appears in the Cyprian cult of the Goddess as her masculine aspect, Aphroditos. [15] The original Hermes had no special need of a love affair with Aphrodite in order to beget Eros with her: he possessed her as his feminine aspect, and perhaps the latter was even the more prominent part before the masculine nature in him became aroused:

Who, though, was the original Goddess, the great *evocatrice*? Cicero passes down two names: Persephone, and the mother of Eros by Hermes, the first Artemis. Properz (II 2, 11) [16] named a third who unites these two to form an original trinitarian image, and he also described the scenery of the primal wedding:

> *Mercurio sacris fertur Boebeidos Undis*
> *virgineum Brimo composuisse latus*

("by the holy waters of Lake Boibeis has Brimo lain her maidenly body at Hermes' side"). Brimo is the Great Goddess of northern Greece, and in the Thessalonian city of Phera she is named Pheraia. She could be equated with Demeter and Persephone on the one hand or with Artemis-Hecate on the other, since she contained all of these in germ-like form within herself. [17] In her territory lies the lake whose name in dialect signifies "owned by Phoebe," and it is therefore the possession of just this "first" Artemis. There she appeared in that elementary sort of maidenliness which does not fear the masculine as something lethally dangerous, but rather challenges, re-quests, and creates it. Granted, this masculinity is a kind "that had no independent personality behind it but was a mere God-servant for the woman," to use the words of the modern author [18] who had deep empathy into feminine nature and who imagined such to be the case for female devotees of a purely phallic God. Just as for Hermes the feminine is nothing more than an opportunity, so for the primal woman he was only an impersonal masculinity, almost a toy.

We may perhaps completely ignore here the descent from Ouranos and Hemera and count it as valid only for Aphrodite. Hermes, the primal lover, is called forth (or brought forth) from the primal woman: he is her own masculine counterpart in the case of the primal Aphrodite, the phallic servant-God in the case of the primal Artemis of Lake Boibeis. All these elements of the seminal situation are contained in the tradition: the Great Goddess, the living primal Herm, and as background something about the primal waters, which in mythological language is the arena of becoming. [19] It may be reasonable to suppose that Hermes' possession in Peloponnesian Pharai of a spring with sacred fish in it, a sort of fishpond, reflects a vague memory of this original scene. [20]   In Arcadia, too, he was honored in the vicinity of swamp and spring. [21] Often the Herms do not simply show the way but indicate where the next spring is to the wanderer. [22]   According to one tradition, the Hermes statue — a very ancient Herm — of the Thracian city Ainos was fished out of the sea. [23]   That the Great Goddess, in the form of Hecate, sometimes took as her lover Hermes, [24]   sometimes the merman Triton, [25] corresponds to such associations of Hermes with bodies of water. But our oldest source, Hesiod, names Hermes just in the passage where he most mightily praises Hecate (*Theog.* 444), and it is just these two who belong most obviously to one another.

Of all the classical manifestations of the primordial Great Goddess who called Hermes into the world as the prototype of the secret lover, Hecate is the most Hermetic. As a messenger (*angelos*) she must be winged, just like her purely celestial *Doppelgängerin*, Iris. Like Hermes, Hecate guides souls; and at crossroads, represented by the Hecataia which were built up on three-cornered pillars, she appears just as out of place in the classical world as do the four-cornered roadside Herms. At every new moon she there received cakes and smoked offerings, as did Hermes. [26] With Hermes she guards the gates and with him, too, brings wealth and good fortune to barns (*Theog.* 444). She has hardly less to do with fruitfulness than has Hermes. Associations with a kind of eroticism that one may find crass and vulgar and a connection to souls and spirits are characteristic for her. [27] The same is the case (and the problem) with Hermes, and with him it is even more problematical since we can now compare father and son also from this angle. On the lofty level of the idealistic, ingenuous Eros, with his passion for self-sacrifice and for reaching out beyond his own life, the union of phallus, soul, and spirit seems conceivable, but on this low, Hecatean level ...? We must recall that the Hermetic essence, seen in his most ancient representations, may only to us appear so low and vulgar, whereas there, where Hecate ruled the world of northern Greece and Thrace [28] in the form of "Aphrodite Zerynthia," it is precisely the crassest that is the holiest and most spiritual.

3   The Mystery of the Herm

Through the mythologem we have discussed above, which is a very ancient
story that Herodotus was already probably hinting at, Hermes, the source of
his own world, was traced back to the source of life itself. More precisely,
he was traced back to a masculine kind of life-source that remains very close
to the feminine, yet only so close that it, being the more active, can still man-
age to bless the other more constant one with two new things: with itself,
and with the continuance of its active nature, the child. This "continuance"
can also be called Eros, but it can be Hermes himself in infant form as it was
in the Hymn. In the Herms the masculine aspect of the life-source does not
appear as blossoming in the child, nor as unfolding in the classical Hermes
image; it appears rather as congealed in its kernel. For this the northern
Greek mythologem could form the text. In point of fact, the traditions of
that story have long since been connected to the reference in Herodotus.[29]
Working directly from the religious life, the historian says that the Athen-
ians were the first of the Greeks to adopt the ithyphallic structure of their
Herms from the Pelasgians, whose cultic practices continued in the mysteries
on Samothrace. In those same mysteries, the enlightening sacred histories
would be related as well (II, 51).

Herodotus is not unsupported in antiquity in his assertion. Kallimachos,
a learned authority on living Greek religion, believed him without needing
to call upon other sources or his own experience. His poem, which began
with a question to an ithyphallic Herm, has not been preserved; we know
only from a summary of the contents that the God who was addressed did

not refer to the fabled Pelasgians but explicitly to the Tyrsenians, the ancient Mediterranian folk who lived on the islands of the Thracian Sea, and to their mystery teachings (*mystikos logos*).[30] Greek scholars and testimonies from the classical and Hellenistic periods confirm that the Herms have an import which was also expressed in a sacred tale, in a mythologem. They describe, too, where both this mode of representation and this mythologem are at home: in Samothrace. The world of northern Greece and Thrace forms a connected geographical area around this island, and this region includes the territory of Lake Boibeis. The mythologem that has its setting at Lake Boibeis can, for internal as well as external reasons, be essentially identical with the sacred story of Samothrace. Perhaps present also in the same place there are related manifestations of the Herm form, which strikes us as so strange.

We call to mind, now, this strange thing, the Herm, not only its ithyphallic form but also its quadratic groundplan: *quod quadratus deus solus habeatur* ("let the four-square God alone possess this"), as was said. The quadratic form, however, calls for a different critical examination than the ithyphallic form with which it is bound up, and only the latter is attributed to the mysteries of Samothrace. The square form that became classical was known in antiquity to be an Athenian invention.[31] In its oldest form, rather broad and more slab than pillar, it may originate in similarly shaped tombstones,[32] but it is not believed that the idea of Hermes developed out of those. If the phallic aspect, though, belongs intrinsically to the Hermes idea, then it could easily enough have drawn tomb and tombstone into its realm. The artist could also have drawn his inspiration from there. But the Herm itself was created only when the pure quadratic form came to prevail in the

67

groundplan. This form is an archetypal expression of totality, inasmuch as
it is rooted in the very foundation of the world. The Greek coin minters un-
consciously, though for that no less symbolically, used this same form as
quadratum-incusum ("the forged square") on the more chthonic side of their
small round works of art.[33] Since the quadratic base is so firmly and chtho-
nically rooted, it fits to the phallic representation. In Arcadia, where the
"Kyllenic style" probably was most authentic, the square structure was especially favored, also for the cultic statues of other Gods. [34] Later it becomes
very commonplace and loses most of its expressiveness. Of the Arcadian Diety
Herms, that of Zeus Teleios in Tegea is significant for understanding the archetypal meaning of this form. Teleios denotes a totality that also incorporates
the chthonic side of being. As an epithet applied to Zeus and Hera, it stands
for the wholeness that is attained in marriage. Through this prototypical (if
not "ideal") marriage pair, this type of wholeness is exemplified for us humans.[35]

From the Greek point of view, the quadratic form as applied to the Herm
is not odd. Also not strange or shocking for the Greeks was the ithyphallic
shape. For the Olympians this was entirely unfitting, except for Hermes,
whom we are trying to understand. In Attica, however, some lesser Gods,
similar to Priapus of the Hellespont, [36] were honored, among them one who
was his equivalent: Tychon. His name means "lucky marksman," one for
whom "having good fortune" (naturally in erotic affairs) is something natural. Of Hermes, who receives this same epithet, one can indeed say that it
hits the mark. [37] And the same applies to his priapic form. Yet, the Athen-
ians distinguished Hermes from such lesser Gods and thought rather of a sa-

cred story from the mysteries which explained this situation for them. Not
only Herodotus and other scholars did this, but the common people did also.
There was a famous statue of "Hermes at the Gate," the *propulaios,* in front
of the propylaeum of the Acropolis, which folk-usage called *amuētos*, "not
a participant in the mysteries."[38] This statue was the work of Alkamenes;
it was a Herm, but one in which the excessive phallus, which reminded Herodotus of the Kabeiroi, was suppressed.[39] The outline that remained did not
appear as a full-fledged sign of a *tetelesmenos* ("inititated one"). We must
consequently follow Herodotus and Kallimachos and approach the mystery
of the Herm in their terms.

In the environs of Samothrace we find (as expected) parallels and allusions
even outside the mysteries, especially if we add to the region of Thrace the
nearby and variously related region of Phrygia. Here appears Priapus, a son
of Hermes according to later traditions. His cult had its home at the Hellespont on ancient Phrygian soil, and from the Greek city states located there
it expanded outward. He constitutes an important parallel not merely because
Hermes is also at work in his activity when he restores virility to the hero of
Petronius' picaresque novel (*Sat.* 140). This simply bespeaks the times and
conforms to the intentionally base level of the novel's style. All the more
significant, though, is that Hermes' guardianship of souls is underscored precisely in this connection and explained as follows: *qui animas ducere et
reducere solet* ("the one who leads souls away and leads them back again").
The Priapus connection is important, too, because he is related to death in
a way that is similar to Hermes. He guards not only gardens but graves.
Wherever he is placed is *mortis et vitai locus,* the place of life and death.
This epigram, which so succinctly and precisely describes his vital place in

69

the realm of death, derives from the time of the first Caesars (CIL, VI, 3708); it agrees, however, with the Phrygian usage of placing phalli an graves as markers.[40]

One famous recent scholar of antiquity did not want to believe in the existence of such tombstones, despite the reports of travelers. Others have considered their form merely accidental and unimportant. It was a step forward when a great archeologist thought to look for some meaning in the most beautiful example of this group of monuments, and we are grateful for the publication of his work.[41] He held that the phallic marker was a symbol of father-right and could originally have belonged only on the graves of men. The image was meant to preserve the virility of the dead man. This explanation moves roughly at the level of Petronius. It is unclear on the point of "father-right symbol," since phallic shapes appeared on the graves of Etruscan men, who may well have been living still in a culture dominated by mother-right.[42] Ir presumes in addition that the meaning which the author ascribes to the marker was forgotten even before the tombstone was created, for the nearly one-meter high stone phallus bears the name and portrait of a woman, "Lysandra of Alexandros."

The mistaken interpretation does not diminish our gratitude to the author who has made public this unique monument from the Museum of Smyrna. For on the condition that one credits it with a vital meaning, it speaks an intelligible language. Set into the lower portion of the mushroom-shaped phallic monument is a Herm. It shows the late form of the Herms, the period of the gravestone being II century B.C.; it is not ithyphallic. Outside on both sides appear two dogs, the animals that accompany the female guide of souls,

Hecate. Present here, then, is the sphere of Hecate-Hermes, into which the realm of Hades can ghost-like discharge itself. In the corona of this lower part the dead woman, waited on by a smaller maiden figure, reigns like a Demeter. From the two sides two winged creatures present her with a garland and a sacred sash. Their butterfly wings identify them as symbolic representations of the soul, as "psyches." To the right of the enthroned woman coils a serpent with head upraised. It reminds us of Demeter's serpent on a frequently found representation of the mystery, which the initiate, who stands before the throne of the Goddess, befriends.[43]

The whole of the monument constitutes a transfigured sphere, accented as spiritual by means of the two psyche figures; it grows upward, as it were, out of the lower parts. These psyche figures, as Curtius noticed, are remarkable in that they are wearing men's clothing, hence are souls of the male sex which are presenting the dead woman there with the symbols of immortality. These masculine psyches are particularly suitable to this monument, which in its totality shows a development and completion of the Herm that is encased in its base. The monument directly poses the question: does not the stone phallus, and with it the Herm, have for the transfigured woman the same meaning as do those masculine souls, as the primary source of immortality on which women draw the same as men? An eternal source of further procreation and life? For this is what the soul would be, as understood from the point of view of its source – the masculine aspect of the life-source.

As source of life, the phallic is related to soul not only in the region of Phrygia; it was so for the Greeks already in archaic times. In other words, seed is also soul. This view appears already on a black-figured Attic vase.[44]

71

There we find a black-bearded man who is blowing on a double flute; he is ithyphallic. Four drops of semen are falling towards a large fluttering butterfly, which itself seems to be the first of the spilled drops. Moreover, on a gem this role of discharging souls is taken by an ithyphallic Herm, which is usually considered to represent Priapus but could just as well be Hermes.[45] Again a butterfly flutters there, and the spiritual atmosphere is emphasized by a peacock on a cistern. On the older Italian gems the blue-gold bird of heaven is a symbol of immortality, and it plays a part in the rebirth story of Ennius.[46] In Greek the butterfly has the same name as soul, *psychē*, but the moth is named *phallaina*, a feminine form of *phallos*, just as *lukaina* ("she-wolf") is the feminine form of *lukos* ("wolf").[47] Although this name (in Latin *phallaena*, from which Italian and Spanish have *falena*) is adapted to the sex of the psyche of the soul-butterfly which is considered to be feminine, it confirms the view that is invoked by the phallic tombstone of Lysandra: the psyche as fluttering moth has a masculine origin. (The double meaning of *psychē*, which probably first meant "soul" and only later "butterfly," is unparalled in any other language.) This is illustrated in the most tangible way possible by the two aforementioned representations. This (butterfly) psyche carries forward something that is masculine, and this is the same sort of immortality which Lysandra is symbolically presented with in the two masculine psyches. Immortality is looked upon here in general, and so too for woman, under the aspect of the active, the masculine.

Which God reigns over this aspect of immortality? Undoubtedly it is Hermes, the phallic and active one. Proceeding from the wider environment of the Samothracian mysteries, we found the meaning of the combination of those factors which otherwise appeared so difficult to understand in the nature of this God. We found this meaning not in a dogma or teaching but in genuine, direct perception, in a truly evident and vivid aspect of the life-source as it is experienced. Such a perception can very well appear in freely floating images – in symbolic representations and in natural objects that are considered as symbols; however, it can also constitute in a crystallized form, the substance of religious celebrations, of mysteries. In any case, behind the symbol – whether it be a natural object, a symbolic representation, or a celebration – a further, fifth dimension opens. The life-source, understood four-dimensionally (physical and temporal) as procreation, has several aspects: a masculine and a feminine, a creative and a lethal. If one insights it, however, through the source of all things, it holds another dimension. Another way of saying it would be that an aspect considered in itself, for instance the masculine as phallus (or, as moth seen as phallus), loses for us the fourth dimension (time) and exchanges it for the fifth; it exchanges the temporal aspect for timeless meaning and for the source that has no beginning, for pure being.

The dimension of time is missing from all the forms of Greek religion, from its cults, its myths, its mysteries. In myth it appears as a special pre-time, out of which time proceeds.[48] Wherever one looks in the world of this religion, the unfettered eye can see primordial meaning and primal source source perceptible in the sulpture of nature.

The main thing that is known to us about the mysteries of Samothrace is that they brought to mind the masculine aspect of this source that continues forever actively working within the human being.[49] According to Herodotus and other witnesses, the Gods who reign on Samothrace, the

Kabeiroi, are just as masculine as the Herms, and they are so in an even more impersonal way since they appear only in groups. In the central shrine of the mystery religion on Samothrace there stood an ithyphallic pair.[50] In an Hermetic-lucky way the aged Goethe divined their essence:

> They are Gods! Wondersome odd,
> Who ever again re-create themselves
> And never know what they are.[51]

This "never knowing" would be the blind phallus, the pure impulse, in contrast to the Hermetic phallus which, in its own special way, is conscious of being so. Goethe's Kabeiroi reach the level of psyche or spirit only by stages; unlike Hermes, they do not have it from the moment of their genesis. Just how things stood on this point in respect to the original, pre-Greek Kabeiroi we shall probably never be able to find out. In the Greek world, the Kabeiroi acquired a state of transparency after the manner of the Greek Gods; sometimes it was of a Dionysian sort, sometimes of a Hermetic. On an eloquent vase-painting from the Kabeiroi shrine at Thebes, the masculine line of the life source descends from Father Kabeiros, continues through his son Pais, then runs on to Pratolaos, the first human, and reaches finally the masculine side of the first pair of lovers — Mitos, the man named "germseed," who signifies unending continuation.[52] The means of mediation between Gods and men, between the original source of souls and the animated creature, is here Dionysian: it passes through the wine goblet before which Pais stands and to which Pratolaos turns his back. Here the Dionysian mode rules, and the father himself, in all his mightiness, is Dionysos.

A different kind of mediation is the Hermetic, that type which comes through the guide of souls and messenger. In the Hymn, Hermes' ambassadorial office was traced back to an initiation ceremony, and in this way he was associated explicitly with the Underworld. The God of the mystery is himself generally the first to be initiated, as Demeter was in Eleusis; there she pre-figured the experience which was then re-experienced and re-lived by her devotees. There can be no further doubt about what mysteries were meant in the Hymn. The Kabeiroi cleansed the *angelos* on the shores of Lake Acheruse and made her a Goddess of the realm of souls. They are Gods of souls, according to their phallic nature. Out of his relation to the Kabeirian nature grows Hermes' role as guardian of souls, which consists in "*ducere et reducere*," and also in his ambassadorial role, which in the Hymn is linked up with his guardianship. This is probably the point where Hermes and the Kabeiroi agree so completely that it was possible for the Herm to be considered the authentic symbol for the Samothracian mysteries. It is as the God of the Kabeirian mysteries that Hermes is ithyphallic and a guide of souls. This is the reason why the phallic aspect was allowed to appear in the Hymn only indirectly, only in the Titanic behavior of the God, and also why the ghostly aspect was only hinted at. This ghostly aspect derives from the source of life being a discharging of souls. Those dwarfish and grotesque – indeed-basically ghostlike and embryonic – figures on the vase paintings of the Theban Kabeirion are only one manifestation of the soul's nature: in this image it stands under the sign of Dionysos and develops in the direction of comedy. The original discharger of souls, however, remains forever the guide of souls, the messenger and herald between the realm of souls and the world of the born.

The great Goddess, who at Lake Boibeis called forth the first discharger of souls, is under many names and guises the mother of souls and mistress of ghosts: as Hecate, as Rhea Kybele (the Near Eastern form of the primal Artemis), as Demeter, as Persephone. As was already pointed out, there are many reasons for identifying the mythologem that was told about her with the sacred story of the Kabeiroi mysteries hinted at by Herodotus. This identification has a genuine probability. Whether the two stories were exactly the same and included the same names is a question that can never be answered. Their correspondence is sufficiently and essentially proven by the fact that the same mythological situation can be established in Samothrace. The great primordial Goddess, called by all the names just mentioned, rules on the island.[53]

The classical mythographic tradition,[54] which deliberately avoids clarity in statements about the mystery Dieties, gives the name Kabeiro to the primordial Mother of the Kabeiroi, and speaks, moreover, of three "Kabeirian nymphs." This tradition breaks down the trinitarian form in the same classical way as does a sculptor when he surrounds a Hecate statue with three dancing maidens and as does another one when he depicts her as three separate, lesser Goddesses and outfits them with the attributes of the Great Goddess.[55] The "Kabeirian nymphs" are related to the Kabeirian Mother in the same way. In Thebes, the Great Goddess Demeter is named Kabiria and proves by this her connection both to the realm of the dead and to the Kabeiroi. In all of these manifestations she is that feminine foundation of the absolute-masculine, of the Kabeiric essence, about which the mythologem of the primal Herm instructed us.

76

It is a soul-realm as the primordial foundation of all actualizations in life that appears here in feminine images: a middle realm between being and non-being and also a foundation for the ambassadorial office. The primordial mediator and messenger moves between the absolute "no" and the absolute "yes," or, more correctly, between two "no's" that are lined up against each other, between two enemies, between woman and man. In this he stands on ground that is no ground, and there he creates the way. From out of a trackless world — unrestricted, flowing, ghostlike — he conjures up the new creation. To him belongs the soul-conjuring wand of the wizard and necromancer, which we so often see in the hand of Hermes. To him also, however, belongs a herald's staff, about which intertwine two antagonistic-loving serpents, a symbol of mediation. In the high archaic period this prototypical image appears as the girdle on the body of the primordial Goddess herself, on the Giant Gorgo in Korfu, who is another form of the original Artemis. Perhaps this appears on the staff of Hermes (the *caduceus*) in the monuments of such a late period because he has his origin in the mystery of mediation between life and death. In Athens one of the carriers of the Eleusinian mysteries had to belong to the family stock of the herald, whose ancestral father was Hermes.[56] Moreover, according to one tradition it was Hermes who together with Daeira (a puzzling manifestation of the original Goddess) begot Eleusis, who was the founder of the mystery-site.[57]

What, then, are the most prominent associations of Hermes to the Kabeirian mysteries? Up to this point we have spoken only of the general features of his Kabeirian nature. To these belonged, first of all, the Herm as a phallic monument. Before we can evaluate the evidence correctly, two

77

more general discussions are necessary. The one has to do with the Herm. To its complete form belongs the head which is borne by the quadratic base; this is symbolic of its self-knowing, self-conscious nature. The name of the God comes, however, from the lower part. Hermeias, contracted as Hermes, is a further development of *herma*, which is the name not of a "stone heap" (*hermax* or *hermaion*, both of them derived from *herma*) but of a single stone, which could be used also as a support or a ship's ballast; the word meant all of these things.[58] The simplest conceivable monument (a phallus-monument) was the primordial symbol of the Kabeirian and Hermetic ideas; this symbol was offered by nature herself.

The Kabeirian idea appeared among the ancient Mediterranean peoples, pre-Greek peoples of the islands and mainland; the Hermes idea appeared among the Greeks. In this way an archetype, in two culturally typical manners,[59] was stimulated to unfold, since the stone pointed to a direct human experience of something divine. Therefore, the "Hermeias" could reveal itself in many places within the realm of Greek culture, even if not always so clearly to everyone as it did to a seer specially chosen by him, a poet of genuine Hermetic spirit. Where the Kabeiroi preceded him with their cult, mythologem, and mystery, the new God could pass as one of them, a Kabeiros who had become spiritually pellucid. But which one of this multitude is Hermes? How can Hermes identify himself with a plurality of figures which at the very least must consist of father and son? This is the second of the broader questions, and we need still to discuss it.

In the masculine principle *per se* — as abstracted from individual persons — the begetter and the begotten are both present; indeed, they are identical.[60] In the mythologem of Aphrodite's birth, the phallus is also the child, just as Hermes is both the Kyllenic monument (the Herm) and the Kyllenic child. This identity receives its most tangible expression in the image of the paternal seed falling to earth in the form of fruit. If we conceive of the soul as masculine, as the eternal seed that is the begetter and procreator, it is also always what is begotten, at once father and son. The ithyphallic pair (as the smallest number) in Samothrace represents the masculine in its minimal unfolding. Of these two, one must be the Kabeirian father, and the various Kabeirian geneologies bear out this assumption. On the often discussed Theban vase-painting we see father and son. Granted, the further development − primordial men and primordial seeds − is also indicated here, but we are not now interested in the Kabeirian precursors of the human race, who follow in the geneologies from the third place onwards. According to the sacred history that Herodotus alludes to, Hermes must be the original begetter. Yet the relevant documentary witnesses equate him explicitly only with the young Kabeiros, the son, named Kasmilos. It never became part of classical tradition that there are two Hermes figures. We recall that the word *eriounios* ("luck-bringer"), which is otherwise an epithet only for Hermes, appears as the name of a pair of chthonic Gods. [61] And on vases we see the old and the young Hermes side by side, both carrying in the same scene the herald's staff.[62] So Kabeirian is this God that he can even appear as a duality.

Tradition has it that one of the islands on which the Kabeiroi were at home, Imbros, belonged jointly to them and to Hermes, and that there he went by the un-Hellenistic name of Imbramos ("the one from Imbros"). This signified a pre-Greek Hermes, who certainly was one of the original Kabeiroi. Here, too, according to one inscription,[63] there were "initiates into the mysteries of Hermes" (*tetelesmenoi Hermēi*). After the foregoing discussion it is superfluous to ask whether Hermes was identical here with Kasmilos; like Hermes, Kasmilos is named among the Kabeiroi on an inscription, and yet he is somewhat removed from them.[64] Hermes was both father and son at the same same time. The situation is similar in the case of Hephaistos as father of the Kabeiroi: under his sign, all the Kabeiroi are *Hephistoi*.[65] The most important evidence, therefore, is to be judged in this light.[66] Following this line of thought, the triad that is narrowly described as Kabeirian would be equivalent to Demeter and Persephone (that is, the primal Goddess under two aspects) and Hades; the fourth figure, who is set apart, Kasmilos, would be equivalent to Hermes. Moreover, in the vase paintings where two Hermes figures show up, one thinks automatically that the elder is Hades, the more paternal spouse of Persephone, and that only the younger one is Hermes.

The ancient Italian testimonies concerning Mercurius correspond extensively to the non-classical tradition concerning Hermes,[67] and they would support what here has been worked out as the God's phallic nature. To go into this would lead us too far astray from our intention of letting the Greek material tell its story. However, one may observe in passing that on Etruscan mirrors Hermes is called *turms aitas*, "Hermes of Hades." This expresses, in the ancient Italian manner, Hermes' chthonic aspect;[68] as well it indicates the Hades-Hermes pair, Kabeirian father and son. The latter was named in Italy also Mercurius Camillus,[69] after Kasmilos, whose role in the Samothracian mysteries is compared by Varro to that of the Roman boy, the *camillus*, at the wedding celebration.[70] Kasmilos-Camillus, the divine boy and the son of a divine father, seems to be the prototype for the sons of holy Roman

80

families, especially for those of the *flamen Dialis* ("high priest of Jupiter").[71]

This unique identification of Hermes with the young Kabeiros corresponds to the classical viewpoint, which already in the *Iliad* has him appear in the form form of a youth. Sculptors of archaic times present him sometimes as bearded, sometimes as youthful; this youthfulness remains always characteristic of him. It is connected originally with Hermes' Kabeirian nature, just as it is also connected to his close relationship to the youths of the palaestra. His youthful image was the only classical-Hellenistic form that was suitable for both the "divine child" and the "son," for the first-born and the first-begotten.[72] His protection of the palaestra is also Kabeiric. He stands there, whether youthful or bearded, as a Kabeirian Eros who strikes us as curious: as the active and manifest original source and at the same time as the prototype of a playfully and nimbly unfolding masculinity.

4 Hermes and the Ram

Have we with Hermes reached right into the mysterious abyss of the active seed? Whether taken literally or symbolically, only these words can define the point from which the world of Hermes opens itself and comes into actual being. Here the question, which we put aside at the beginning of our inquiry, crops up: "How could just this appear to the Greeks as *God*? " We are referring not to the world of Hermes but rather to its origin. We are not speaking of the phallus, but literally of something abysmal, of something that is active from the pre-historic depths, whose symbolization as given by nature itself − every bodily organ also expresses its meaning − is this so-called fertility symbol. If this is indeed the way these things are related, then the question proves to be unnecessary, and what remains for us is to show the depths that open for us with Hermes wherever they make themselves noticeable in the monuments.

A unique report has come down to us that relates to an area which lies in closest proximity to the mysteries: the family cult, [73] or in any case a cult that was practiced in the innermost part of the Greek home. Here occurs the first mention of the hermaphrodite in the literature. Theophrastus characterizes the superstitious person, among others, in the following sketch:

> "On the fourth and seventh day of the month
> he has wine cooked at home, goes out and buys
> myrtle branches, incense, and offering cakes,
> and returns home where he crowns the hermaphrodites
> with garlands the whole day through." [74]

Does the exaggeration consist only in saying that the superstitious person

82

did this every fourth and seventh day of the month and for the whole day, or does it also lie in saying that in the innermost part of his house stood not only one but several statues of the hermaphrodite? Was the presence of at least one hermaphroditic statue within the house just as common as a Hermes and a Hecate out in front of the house, in the yard, or at the gateway to the road? Unfortunately we know too little about the Greek house-cult to be able to answer this with certainty, either affirmatively or negatively. This much, though, seems to be certain, that all three kinds of divine statue belonged among the relics of the house that were inherited from the ancestors; they belonged to the "paternal," and possibly also the "maternal," Gods.[75] These were, in any case, related to the origins of the family: they represented the inexhaustible source of life and souls from which the family continued to originate over and over again. And, indeed, the hermaphrodite within the house represents so to speak the origin of the source: he represents the primal condition restored in marriage, the one who precedes even the genesis of the first Herm and the generation of souls. It is not without good reason that a widow is found imploring the hermaphrodite in a small Attic temple dedicated to him:[76] she is expecting from him restoration of that condition which is far more than transient happiness in love or mere amorous union. Even today the Greeks call the married couple *to androgyno*, "the androgene."

The position of the Herm at the entrance — whether in the yard or on the road[77] — is that of the mediator. Hermes' connection to the center of the house, to the Goddess of the hearth, is attested by a Homeric Hymn to Hestia (**XXIX**). Every now and then he appears in this "innermost nook:" Kallimachos tells how, blackened by smoke, he bounds up from there to frighten divine maidens (*Hymn.* 3, 69). Those "innermost nooks" include the bridal chamber and bedroom, and there, according to a tradition from Euboia, Hermes rules as *Epithalamitēs.*[77a] The Kabeirian guide of souls is at work both within the house and without. He guides souls out of his realm — the world of paths and roads — back into the warm life of the household, which in Greek signifies the "family." In his official capacity as mediator between the worlds of night and day, spirits and men, and (standing before the temple) between the worlds of Gods and mankind, he is called *Propylaios* ("before the gate") and *Pylaios* ("before or at the gate").[78] This is not only because a thief is the best doorkeeper![79] One inscription names him *Pylaios* ("the one at the entrance") and *Harmateus* ("driver of the chariot"). Two other epithets — *strophaios* ("standing at the door-post," also "cunning," "versatile") and *stropheus*[80] (the "socket" in which the pivot of the door moves) — show him closely related to door hinges and therefore to the entrance, but also to a middle point, to the socket, about which revolves the most decisive issue, namely the alternation life-death-life.

So little about the Hermes festivals has been handed down in the tradition because they have to do with the most secret source and pivot-point of human existence. There were few temples of Hermes,[81] moreover, just because that crucial issue was felt wherever people lived and died. Through Hermes, every house became an opening and a point of departure to the paths that come from far off and lead away into the distance. Standing at the doorway, he indicates that here is a source of life and death, a place where souls break in, as though he were pointing out a spring of fresh water. At a Hermes festival on Crete,[82] the "low ones," the slaves, were elevated and served by their masters. At another festival on Samos[83] — the feast of Hermes Charidotes — the populace was allowed to steal and to commit highway robbery. Everywhere that Hermes appears, even when it is as "guardian," there is an influx and invasion from the underworld. This is not an invasion of death but rather, to coin a phrase, of "underworldly life." To this belong all the "serving spirits," that whole "service industry," which Hermes represents in several forms. The inversion of the master-slave relationship has its nearest parallel in the Roman Saturnalia, a winter solstice festival, whose meaning was the strengthening of the weakest in that wonderful growth that one re-experiences with the sun after having already experienced it as seed and embryo. That which hovers between being and non-being, seemingly powerless, repressed in servitude, reduced to the life in the nocturnal darkness of the seed, finds its way upward. Hermes, the psychopomp, also called Harmateus, the "soul-carrier," guides it, brings it back ...

An ancient manifestation of Hermes points particularly to the parallelism between the leading upward of the soul and of the sun. At the festival of Tanagra, the only festival of Hermes whose sacred rituals — they were dedicated to eliciting the God's presence — are intimately familiar to us, the handsomest youth carried a ram on his shoulders around the city's walls. He did this in imitation of the God who is said to have driven off a pestilential illness in this manner.[84] The image of ram-bearer (*Kriophoros*), as Hermes is so often portrayed,[85] is a highly significant manifestation. The story that Hermes had performed this act for exactly this purpose may be a later addition to the mythologem; this becomes plainly apparent in its basic features — the epiphany with the ram and the circumambulation — and is hardly to be segregated from the further connections of Hermes to the ram.[86] As a sacrificial animal and theriomorphic expression, the ram belongs generally within the Kabeirean context.[87] When Hermes begot Saos, the founding hero of Samothrace, with Rhene (the "sheep"),[88] he certainly did so in the guise of a ram. A whole series of gem pictures shows him as a ram with one or more — in one case even with four — other rams.[89] Unmistakable, too, is the sacred history of the mother-mysteries, to which Pausanias alludes (II, 3, 4); what is said there about Hermes and the ram Pausanias knows, but will not reveal. As a ram, Hermes begets the divine child of the mysteries, who though he is not merely the sun[90] yet does resemble the new-born sun, and as son of the ram-father is also presumably the lamb (or the ram) which Hermes brings and carries around the neighborhood, thereby making him a sun-bearer of the new sun. It is not without good reason that the golden rams of saga are gifts of Hermes. As is well known, he gives such sunlike animals to the house of Atreus and to Phrixos.[91]

We did not wish to consider the depths of Hermes, and yet they have themselves led us, on a truly Hermetic path, far in this direction. From a purely historical investigation, our inquiry has led to the pre-historical ram-God, whose form was taken not only by Hermes but also by his brother Apollo, who as a primal child was also a small sun.[92] Granted, this figure is not in the classical Greek manner. Its lack of refinement can perhaps be best adduced in a crude ram-headed Herm that was found in the neighborhood of Gythion.[93] In this city, located in southern Peloponnesus, there was at the end of the second century A.D. a temple for the ram-headed sun-God of the Egyptians, Ammon (Pausanias III, 21, 8). In addition, a cult statue of Apollo Karneios testifies that this God was formerly worshipped in this same place. His epithet stems from *karnos*, a pre-Greek word for livestock,[94] which in Greece always meant primarily sheep. Here the later Apollo is preceded by a ram-God, whose former, old-Mediterranean importance is verified by the fact that Ammon — most likely an ancient relative — settled finally in just this cultic spot. Carna, who in Rome bears the feminine form of the name Karnos, was a moon-Goddess[95]; with Janus, in whom the Romans[96] rightly knew a sun-God and whom they equated with Apollo,[97] she formed a couple, as is typical of sun and moon personifications in other mythologies. Hermes is never named Karneios, and his dual relation to the ram — as father and as bearer — does not indicate a simple identity with the sun. He is not the source of light, as the sun is, but rather the source of this source. He also begot the moon-like and dark Pan. His world originates before sunrise, and as the source of his world he can only be the one who himself allows a source of illumination to originate in the outpouring of souls. Is not, then, the sun re-born in every soul that is newly guided upward, just as it is in every drop of water that mirrors it? Under the aspect of Hermes, however, the sun belongs to the soul more essentially than it does to a mirror, where it is accidental. In the prehistoric depths of the life-source, light and its mirror are begotten simultaneously; there, as great Greek philosophers also knew, the source of light and the source of soul are one and the same.

5 *Silenos and Hermes*

It is not without good reason that Hermes was supposed to be the inventor of language.[98] It belongs to the Hermetic wisdom of the Greek language itself, to one of its most ingenious chance hits, that the word for the simplest mute stone monument, *herma*, from which the name of the God stems, corresponds phonetically to the Latin *sermo*, "speech" or any verbal "exposition".[98a] The word *herma*, which in the Greek does not have this meaning, does however form the basic verbal root for *hermēneia*, "explanation." Hermes is *hermēneus* ("interpreter"), a linguistic mediator, and this not merely on verbal grounds. By nature he is the begetter and bringer of something light-like, a clarifier, God of ex-position and inter-pretation (of the kind also that we are engaged in) which seeks and in his spirit — the spirit of the shameless ex-position of his parents' love affair — is led forward to the deepest mystery.

For the great mystery, which remains a mystery even after all our discussing and explaining, is this: the appearance of a speaking figure, the very embodiment as it were in a human-divine form of clear, articulated, play-related and therefore enchanting, language — its appearance in that deep primordial darkness where one expects only animal muteness, wordless silence, or cries of pleasure and pain. Hermes the "Whisperer" (*psithyristēs*)[99] inspirits the warmest animal darkness. His epiphany supplements the Silenos aspect of the life-source, in which the animalistic factor within the Greek pantheon shows its presence, and within it forms a fundamental harmony and totality.

Hermes and Silenos — or the Silenoi (plural) — harmonize in their phallic nature more than just superficially. The brilliant messenger of the Gods, whom Praxiteles represented in the famous statue of Olympia, carried the child Dionysos on his arm, a task ordinarily left to the "teacher of Dionysos," the old Silenos.[100] Just why Hermes can appear in this role was made comprehensible to us through the meaning of Kriophoros. He is the designated bearer of all divine children,[101] since he is the bringer of souls and of sun-children. His relation to Dionysos again comes to light in his designation as a God of the vineyards on the island of Lesbos. Silenos, or Hermes, with the little Dionysos form a kind of variation on the same theme, and are the two sides of the same reality. The supreme knowledge of the Greeks, not however expressed in conceptual terms, that the Hermetic-spiritual aspect exists in friendly union with the animal-divine aspect, is revealed most beautifully on a wonderful vase-painting. This conjunction occurs there most likely without the artist intending it. Nevertheless, it will still best summarize our reflections.

We recall that the Homeric Hymn to Aphrodite mentions Hermes with the Silenoi as lovers of the nymphs. It is another thing altogether when a London vase, a so-called Psykter of the painter Duris, dating from the first quarter of the fifth century[102] shows a whole troop of frisky Silenoi, some of them ithyphallic, whose leader — the eldest of a Satyr choir, as it were — appears with the emblems of Hermes: the traveler's mantel and the herald's staff. We must linger at this picture before moving on to another more comprehensive one. Here no nymphs are apparent. Drunkenness and wine goblets, with which the figures playfully move about, indicate the half-bestial, half-divine devotees of Dionysos. But why the presence here of Hermes in the leading Silenos? It is believed that this picture reflects the choir of a Satyr drama performing some specific role, similar to the ambassadorial role of Hermes in whose place the satyr choir was commissioned, as for instance to lead Hephaistos back up to Olympus. This is one possibility, but there is another. The appearance of Silenoi, as devotees of Dionysos, would be in itself most natural during the Dionysian soul-festival in the month of Anthesterion [the eighth month of the Attic year, corresponding to end of February-beginning of March. -Tr.]. A noted scholar of religion held the Silenoi and Satyrs to be the spirits themselves, the souls of the dead.[103] He erred perhaps only in that the identification of Satyrs and Silenoi with the souls of the dead has no evidence to back it up and goes against the pictorial imagination. But from this point of departure, we recognize what these figures represent: the source of life which is opened up and is discharging itself. The days of the Anthesteria ("Feast of the Flowers") were open days for the souls, and the fifth and last of them, *chytroi* ("feast of the pots"), was a Hermes day.[104] On this day the identical meaning of the Silenic nature and the office of soul-leader may have manifested itself through the Hermes costume.

Concerning the actual picture we are here dealing with, it is not merely a matter of conjectural possibilities. We are speaking of a Berlin amphora, dating from the same period as the Psykter of Duris, whose craftsman is usually named after this piece. A connoisseur of Greek vase-painting characterizes the artist in the following way: "The slender elegance of his dynamic figures that embellish rather than narrate a tale never attained in its quiet poetry such a pure form as in the figures of the Berlin vase."[105] Here the choir disappears completely from the observer's vantage point; whether or not it remains in the background is unimportant. Before us stands a unique pair: Silenos and Hermes. The delicate figure of a deer between them hints at the untamed world which has been rendered tractable by Dionysian magic, and this highly significant divine playing takes place on a surface that is etched with the lines of eternal rhythm, the spirals.[106] So far as we can surmise, this is not a scene from a Satyr drama. Even if it were so, the facial features would tell everything – the bestial yet grave face of the one and the super-humanly intelligent head of the other, and despite this difference the inter-fusion of their essential forms. Silenos has the lyre and lyre-pick of Hermes, while Hermes, behind him almost like a *Doppelgänger* yet clearly marked by his winged hat and shoes, holds the Dionysian vessel of Silenos in his hand. They have exchanged roles, and this was allowed because at bottom, where Hermes is merely a Kabeiros, they have one and the same function: the con-juring of luminous life out of the dark abyss that each in his own way is.

It was the Hermetic tune, an unforgettable melody of Greek mythology, that with all its variations from the Kabeiroi-Silenoi aspects to the role of the speech-gifted mediator and psychogogue was to resound in these reflections. Whoever does not shy away from the dangers of the most pro-found depths and the newest pathways, which Hermes is always prepared to open, may follow him and reach, whether as scholar, commentator, or phi-losopher, a greater find and a more certain possession. For all to whom life is an adventure – whether an adventure of love or of spirit – he is the com-mon guide. *Koinos Hermes!*

91

NOTES AND REFERENCES

PREFACE

1 Quoted from *Mythology and Humanism — The Correspondence of Thomas Mann and Karl Kerényi*, transl. Alex. Gelley (Ithaca, Cornell University Press, 1975), p. 9.

2 Bollingen Series LXV, Princeton University Press.

3 K. Kerényi, *Werkausgabe* (München, Langen-Müller, 1967), Bd. II, p. 69.

4 *Ibid.*, p. 63.

5 *Werkausgabe* Bd. III., p. 198.(italics — M. K.).

6 *Briefwechsel aus der Nähe: Hermann Hesse/Karl Kerényi* (München, Langen-Müller, 1972), p. 120.

7 Rhein-Verlag, Zürich.

8 Letter to Thomas Mann, Dec. 21, 1944, *op. cit. sup.*, p. 106.

NOTES AND REFERENCES

PART ONE

1 Walter F. Otto, *The Homeric Gods*, New York (Pantheon), 1954, translated by Moses Hadas. (The translations of quotations from the German original of this work are, unless otherwise indicated, my own. The Hadas translation has, however, been consulted. -Tr.)

2 Cf. Kerenyi, *Der grosse Daimon des Symposion,* Albae Vigiliae XIII, Amsterdam, 1942, p. 32f; in "Humanistische Seelenforschung" *Werke in Einzelausgaben,* vol. I, München 1966, pp. 306ff.

3 Cf. Jung-Kerényi, *Essays on a Science of Mythology*, Bollingen Series XXII, Princeton (Princeton Univ. Press), 3rd ed., 1971 (paperback), p. 127.

4 Cf. Hesych. *s.v. ktéres*; Solmsen, *Indog. Forsch.* 3, p. 96f; C.v. Ostergaard, *Hermes* 38, pp. 333ff; H. Güntert, *Kalypso*, Halle, 1919, p. 162f.

5 Cf. Kerényi, *The Religion of the Greeks and Romans* (hereinafter *Greeks & Romans*), transl. C. Holme, London (Thames & Hudson), 1962, p. 199; 3rd ed. Greenwood Reprinting, 1973. Originally titled *Die antike Religion*, Amsterdam/Leipzig (Pantheon), 1941.

6 This is especially striking in Book II, 104, where the text does *not* read, "Zeus sent the scepter through Hermes to Pelops," but rather that Zeus gave it to Hermes, Hermes to Pelops, Pelops to Atreus, etc.

7 Cf. Kerényi, *Apollon*, Vienna/Leipzig, 1937, p. 128ff; enl. ed. Düsseldorf, 1953, p. 123ff.

8 Preller-Robert, *Griechische Mythologie* I, Berlin, 1894, p. 421,

9 Hesiod, *Fragments*, 112 (Rzach); Servius in Verg., *Aenead* II, 79.

10 Cf. my treatment of the Hymn to Hermes in Jung-Kerényi, *op. cit.,* pp. 51ff.

93

NOTES AND REFERENCES

11 *The Homeric Hymns*, translated by Andrew Lang, London, 1899. -Tr.
(The author acknowledges his debts to W. Allen and E. E. Sikes, *The Homeric
Hymns*, London, 1904; Th. v. Scheffer, *Die homerischen Götterhymnen*, Jena,
1927; and L. Radermacher, "Der homerische Hermeshymnus," *Sitz.-Ber. Wien*
213, 1, 1931.

12 Cf. Hesych. *s.v. ounei*; Th. Bergk, Philol. 11, p. 384; Radermacher, *op. cit.* on
this passage; C. M. Bowra, *J. Hell. Stud.* 54, p. 68.

13 Antoninus Liberalis, 25.

14 Cf. Jung-Kerényi, pp. 106ff.

15 The ancient interpreters already emphasized the stolen love. Cf. Schol. in Hom.
Il. XXIV 24; for modern interpretations, cf. S. Eitrem, *Philologus* 65, 1906
p. 249.

16 Cf. Kerényi, *Apollon, op. cit.*, pp. 136ff; 3. ed. p. 129ff.

17 Cf. W. Schmidt, "Geburtstag im Altertum," *Religionsgesch. Versuche und Vorarbeiten* VII, 1, Giessen, 1908.

18 Preller-Robert, *op. cit.*, p. 391.

19 Lykophr. 680. Harpocr. *s.v.* A four-headed Hermes stood at the intersection
of three roads in Kerameikos, Hesych. *s.v. trikēphalos*. This shows that it is not
based on the *number* of roads.

20 Cf. Jung-Kerényi, p. 57.

21 Suidas, Photius, *Etym. Magn. s.v. hermaion*.

22 Cf. Jung-Kerényi, pp. 57ff. The tortoise also has a connection to Aphrodite:
Phidias places the Goddess atop this animal, cf. Plutarch, *Conjug. praec.* VII, 421.

23 The passage alluded to here reads in the Odyssey: " ...I too hear sounding the

lyre, which the Gods make the friend of feasts." This parallel is important because it heightens even more the irony of Hermes' words; the hearer is allowed through this technique to feel the insincere usage of flowery language.

24 Kerényi, *Greeks & Romans, op. cit.,* 193ff.

25 Cf. Radermacher on this passage.

26 Otto, *op. cit.,* pp. 111ff; also Jung-Kerényi, p. 54.

27 Cf. P. Philippson, *Genealogie als mythische Form,* Symbolae Osloenses 7, 1936.

27a Cf. Kerényi, *Apollon,* p. 110; 3. ed. p. 109.

27b Cf. Otto, *op. cit.,* pp. 33 & 106; Kerényi, *Greeks & Romans, op. cit.,* p. 198f.

27c Cf. Kerényi, *Greeks & Romans,* pp. 181ff.

28 The word *phonēs* was handed down by tradition. The correction is by G. Hermann; besides its better sense, it recommends itself because the word appears again in v. 385, where the famous Moscow script (in Leiden) has *phorēn,* the others *phonēn.*

29 In the Hymn they seem to appear as rivals – cf. Eitrem, *op. cit. sup.* This is however only superficial appearance: a divine foreplay preceding the division of territories, not a competition between cults.

30 Cf. S. Eitrem, *Hermes und die Toten,* Christiania Videnskabs-Selskabs Forhandlinger, 1909, 5, p. 24f.

30a Cf. Kerényi, *Apollon,* p. 166f; 3. ed. p. 152f.

30b Horace, *Carm.* II 7, 13; 17, 29; *Sat.* II 6, 15; Kerényi, *Apollon,* p. 218f; 3. ed. p. 217f.

31 Cf. Kerényi, *Greeks & Romans,* p. 198f.

NOTES AND REFERENCES

32　The underworldly meaning of his service as shepherd to King Admetus, whose queen has a Persephone-Demeter-Hecate form, is also supported by this connection. On Apollo's dark features, cf. *Apollon, op. cit.,* pp.48ff; 3. ed. p. 43f.

33　So it stands in the legends of Pindar's and Plato's childhoods. According to Pindar (*Ol.* 6, 45ff.), the Iamos received the gift of prophesy through serpents nourishing him with honey. For a collection of examples, cf. A. B. Cook, *Hell. Stud.* 15, pp. 1ff.

34　Vergil, *Georg.* IV, 219ff.

35　On honey as food of the Gods, cf. H. Usener, "Milch und Honig," *Kleine Schriften* IV, p. 400. Cf. also Radermacher on this passage of the Hymn, where further literature on this theme can be found.

36　Cf. the entry in Pauly-Wissowa, *Realenc.* VIII, p. 784; also *sortes Mercurii,* F. Altheim, *Griech. Götter im alten Rom, Versuche und Vorarbeiten* XXII, 1, 1930, p. 74.

37　Schol. in Theocr. II 11, 12; G. Kaibel, *Com. Graec. fragm.* I, p. 161. The story by which this initiation of the *angelos* is established belongs to a more recent layer of the mythological account, but it does not follow from this that what is established is not itself much older. On the connection of Hecate to the Kabeiroi, cf. Kerényi, *Das Aegäische Fest*, Albae Vigiliae XI, Amsterdam, 1941, p. 67; 4. ed. in *Werkausg.*, vol. I, München, 1966, p. 140.

38　Porphyry in Hor. *Carm.* I 10, 9.

39　The first was the postulation of L. Curtius, *Die antike Herme*, Diss. München, 1903. The second was that of L. Deubner, *Der ithyphallische Hermes*, Stuttgart, 1937, pp. 201ff. Deubner speaks of a "God of the road," though what he means is no more than the spirit of the signpost: "From the signpost grew the God of the road" (p. 203).

39a　With thanks to Armin Kesser (Zürich) for having pointed out the accord between Moritz and myself.

NOTES AND REFERENCES

40   Otto, *op. cit.,* pp. 118-20.

41   *Ibid.,* p. 120.

42   An exception is that of the Danaides, who murdered their men on the wedding
      night and through that offended Hermes, who is the Epithalamites, the pro-
      tector of the bridal chamber. They had, therefore, to be cleansed through him.
      Apollod. *Bibl.* II 1, 5, 11.

PART TWO

1   Plato, *Symposium,* in *The Collected Dialogues,* edited by Edith Hamilton
      & Huntington Cairns, Bollingen Series LXXI, New York, 1961, pp. 555-56.

1a   Cf. Kerényi, *Der grosse Daimon,* p. 14ff; in *Werkausg.,* vol. I, pp. 293ff.

2   Compare P. Philippson, *Genealogie als mythische Form,* op. cit., p. 16.

3   Jung-Kerényi, p. 53.

4   *Ibid.,* p. 55, and *Der grosse Daimon,* pp.34f., resp. 308f.

5   Cf. Kerényi, *Der grosse Daimon,* pp. 23ff., 36f; in *Werkausg.,* vol. I, pp. 300ff.,
      309f.

6   Cf. Kerényi, *Apollon,* p. 218; 3. ed., p. 217.

7   Cf. these passages in Allen-Sikes.

8   Preller-Robert, *op. cit.,* I, p. 323; cf. Plutarch, *De aud. poet.* 44e.

NOTES AND REFERENCES

9   From the second half of the fifth century. Cf. L. R. Farnell, *The Cults of the Greek States* V, Oxford, 1909, Plate IV.

10 ˙ Cf. Jung-Kerényi, pp. 112-115.

11   On Cicero's source, see J. B. Mayor's edition, Cambridge, 1885, III, pp. 199ff. & 205.

12   Cicero, *De nat. deor.* III 22, 56; *Mercurius unus Caelo patre, Die matre natus, cuius obscenius excitata natura traditur, quod aspectu Proserpinae commotus sit.*

13   Cf. Jung-Kerényi, p. 53.

14   *Ibid.*, p. 56.

15   *Ibid.*, p. 54.

16   Based upon Turnebus' good conjectural reading of the text: *Brimo* in place of
_ the meaningless *primo.*

17   Cf. Jung-Kerényi, pp. 120ff.

18   D. H. Lawrence, *Lady Chatterley's Lover.*

19   Cf. Jung-Kerényi, pp. 46ff.

20   Pausanias, VII 22, 4; and Jung-Kerényi, p. 55.

21   At Pheneos and Stymphalos; see Farnell, *op. cit.,* V, p. 80.

22   Cf. U. v. Wilamowitz-Moellendorf, *Hellenistische Dichtung,* II, Berlin, 1924, p. 102f.

23   Kallimachos, *Diegeseis* (Norsa & Vitelli), Florence, 1934, VII, pp. 32ff.

NOTES AND REFERENCES

24 She bore him three daughters: Schol. in Lyc. *Alex.* 680.

25 He conceived Krataiis with her: Schol. in Hom. *Od.* XII, 124; Theopomp in Porphyry's *On Abstinence*, II, 16.

26 Preller-Robert, *op. cit.*, I, pp. 322, 402.

27 Cf. Kerényi, *Apollon*, p. 157; 3. ed. pp. 145f.

28 Cf. Kerényi, *Das Aegäische Fest*, p. 67; in *Werkausg.* vol. I, p. 140.

29 Cf. C. A. Lobeck, *Aglaophamus*, II, Königsberg, 1829, p. 1213.

30 Kallimachos, *Diegeseis*, VIII 33ff; cf. IV 1.

31 Pausanias, I 24, 3 and IV 33, 3.

32 L. Curtius, "Die antike Herme," pp. 7ff. (and against R. Lullies, *Die Typen der griechischen Herme*, Königsberg, 1931, p. 42) in *Die Wissenschaft am Scheidewege von Leben und Geist, Klages-Festschrift,* Leipzig, 1932, pp. 26, 9.

33 Cf. Kerényi-Lanckoronski, *Der Mythos der Hellenen in Meisterwerken der Münzkunst*, Amsterdam/Leipzig, 1941, pp. 21ff; in *Werkausg.*, vol. I, p. 211.

34 M. W. De Visser, *Die nicht menschengestaltigen Götter der Griechen,* Leiden, 1903, p. 23 and the entry in *Realenc.* VIII, Pauly-Wissowa, pp. 704ff.

35 This important fact completely eluded H. Bolkenstein in his *"Telos ho gamos," Mededeel. Konink. Akad. Wetensch. Afd. Letterk. Deel* 76, Series B., No. 2., Amsterdam, 1933. There also, quite unintentionally, he seeks to weaken the testimony of ancient scholars. The most complete collection of their remarks is to be found in his article.

36 Cf. H. Herter, *De dis Atticis Priapi similibus*, Diss. Bonn, 1926.

NOTES AND REFERENCES

37 Otto, *Homeric Gods, op. cit.*, p. 111.

38 Cf. Preller-Robert, I, p. 402.

39 "Beneath the head of the *propulaios*, which Alkemenes completed, one can no longer think of the ithyphallus," says Wilamowitz in *Der Glaube der Hellenen* I, Berlin, 1931, p. 162. Noteworthy is the inner inscription on the copy found in Pergamon: *GNOTHI SAUTON*, that is, "know thyself," the divine-human in you.

40 H. Herter, *"De Priapo," Religionsgesch. Versuche u. Vorarbeiten* XXIII, Giessen, 1932, pp. 232 & 229.

41 L. Curtius, in *Klages-Festschrift, op. cit.*, pp. 19ff.

42 Cf. E. Altheim, *Epochen der röm. Gesch.*, Frankfurt a/M., 1934, pp. 234ff.

43 Cf. Farnell, *op. cit.*, III, Plate XVa, of the Urna Lavatelli in Rome.

44 Cf. H. Güntert, *Kalypso*, Halle, 1919, for further references.

45 Cf. Herter, *"De Priapo," op. cit.*, pp. 134, 160f.

46 Cf. Kerényi, *Pythagoras und Orpheus*, Albae Vigiliae II, Amsterdam, 1940, p. 57.

47 Cf. O. Immisch, *Glotta* 6, 1915, pp. 193ff. Also, Güntert, *op. cit.*, p. 220.

48 Cf. P. Philippson's pioneering work, *Zeitart des Mythos* in *Untersuchungen über den Griechischen Mythos*, Zürich, 1944, pp. 43ff.

49 Cf. Kerényi, *Der grosse Daimon*, pp. 29ff; *Werkausg.*, vol. I, pp. 304ff.

50 Hippolytus, *Refutatio Haer.*, V, 8, 9.

51 Goethe, *Faust* II, 8075ff. Cf. Kerényi, *Das Aeg. Fest*, pp. 58ff; *Werkausg.*, vol. I, pp. 133ff.

NOTES AND REFERENCES

52 Pictured in Wolters-Bruns, *Das Kabirenheiligtum bei Theben*, Berlin, 1940, Plate 5.

53 Cf. Preller-Robert, *op. cit.,* I, pp. 328, 4; 851, 2; 856f.

54 Akusilaos of Argos and Pherekydes of Athens, both of the fifth century B. C. Cf. also the passage by O. Kern in Pauly-Wissowa, *Realenc.* X, pp. 1399ff.

55 Cf. E. Petersen, *Archäol.-epigr. Mittheil. aus Oesterreich* 5, 1881, pp. 26ff. and 32ff.

56 Cf. Preller-Robert, *op. cit.,* I, p. 411, 1.

57 Pausanias, I 38, 7.

58 *Herma*, however, never meant "Herm," for this is expressed in Greek by "Hermes" or "small Hermes," *hermidiōn.*

59 Cf. original German edition of Jung-Kerényi, *Einführung in das Wesen der Mythologie*, Amsterdam/Leipzig (Pantheon), 1941, p. 37, n. 1, which question has been further elaborated by the author in "Archetypisches und Kultur-typisches in der Griechischen und Römischen Religion," *Paideuma* (Frankfurt a/M.) V, 3, 1951, pp. 98-102.

60 Cf. Jung-Kerényi, p. 56.

61 Antoninus Liberalis, 25.

62 Furtwängler-Reichhold, *Italisch-ionische Amphora aus Vulci* (Munich) Plate 21; Gerhard, *Etruskischer Stamnos* (Museo Gregoriano) CCXL. It is to O. Froebe-Kapteyn that we owe our appreciation of the importance of these vase paintings.

63 Farnell, *op. cit.,* V, p. 80.

64 *Ibid.,* p. 81.

NOTES AND REFERENCES

65 Cf. Photius *s.v.*

66 Schol. in Apoll. Rhod., *Arg.* I, 917, following Mnaseas and Dionysodoros.

67 As expected from Altheim's research. Cf. his *Griech. Götter im Alten Rom*, pp. 39ff. on Mercurius.

68 Kerényi, *Studi e Mat. di Storia delle Rel.* 9, 1933, pp. 17ff.

69 Altheim, *op. cit.,* p. 82.

70 *De lingua Lat.* VII 34.

71 Cf. Kerényi, *Greeks & Romans, op. cit.,* pp. 219ff.

72 Cf. Jung-Kerényi, p. 66.

73 Cf. Kerényi, *Der grosse Daimon*, p. 28; *Werkausg.,* vol. I, p. 303.

74 Theophrastus, *Charact.* 16, 10.

75 H. Bolkenstein, "Theophrastos' Character der Deisidaimonia als religionsge-schichtliche Urkunde," *Religionsgesch. Versuche und Vorarbeiten* XXI, 2, Giessen, 1929, pp. 45ff. His further inferences rest upon a misunderstanding of the mythological character of the hermaphrodite.

76 Alciphr., *Epist.* 3, 37.

77 Cf. Eitrem in Pauly-Wissowas, *Realenc.* VII 701, § §4 & 6.

77a Hesych. *s.v.*

78 Cf. Farnell, *op. cit.,* V, p. 66, and especially the Pythagorean interpretation of Diogenes Laertius VIII, 1, 31, which explicitly connects this attribute of Hermes to his leadership of souls. According to Pythagoras he is *tamias psychōn,* "steward of souls." Cf. Kerényi, *Pythagoras und Orpheus,* p. 12.

NOTES AND REFERENCES

79 As in the conception of late antiquity (Suidas, "strophaion"). The same with Aristoph. Plut. 1153, and the related "stropheus" (Photius).

80 From Erythrai in Asia Minor, Farnell, *op. cit.*

81 M. P. Nilsson, *Griech. Feste von religiöser Bedeutung mit Ausschluss der Attischen*, Leipzig, 1906, p. 388.

82 Athen. VI, 263F and XIV, 639B.

83 Plutarch, *Quaest. Graec.* 55.

84 Pausanias IX 22, 1; W. F. Otto, *Dionysus*, Bloomington, Ind., 1965, p. 42f.

85 Cf. Höfer's article, in Roscher, *Ausführl. Lex. der griech. u. röm. Mythologie* II, pp. 1431ff.

86 Cf. Eitrem, *Beiträge z. griech. Religionsgeschichte* I: "Der vor-dorische Widder-gott," Christiania Videnskabs–Selskabs Forhandl., 1910, 4, pp. 5ff.

87 Cf. V. Fritze, *Zeitschr. f. Numism.*, 24, pp. 111ff.

88 Schol. in Apoll. Rhod., I, 917; Diod. V, 48.

89 Eitrem, *op. cit.,* pp. 4ff.

90 For this principle, cf. Jung-Kerényi, p. 45.

91 Euripides, *Orestes*, 1.997; Apollod. *Bibl.* I 9, 1.

92 Besides Eitrem, *op. cit.,* cf. O. Wide and Höfer in Roscher, *op. cit.* II, pp. 961ff.

93 A. B. Cook, *Zeus*, I, Cambridge, 1914, p. 351.

103

NOTES AND REFERENCES

94 This follows P. Kretschmer's remarks in *Glotta* 21, 88. It is also possible that the Greek word is of Illyrian origin and relates to the old Irish *carn* ("pile of stones"). Thus the cult of the ram and the stone monument could be intimately connected to the pre-indogermanic religious heritage of several indogermanic peoples. Cf. Etruscan *carna*-names hinted at by R. Pettazoni, *Studi Etruschi* 14, p. 172.

95 R. Pettazzoni, *Studi Etruschi* 14, pp. 163ff.

96 *Ibid.*, p. 171; Murbach's article in Pauly-Wissowa, *Realenc.* III, A, p. 902; O. Huth, *Janus*, Bonn, 1932; Altheim, "Die Sonne in Kult und Mythos," *Wörter und Sachen*, N. F. 1.

97 Cf. Börtzler, "Janus und seine Deuter," *Schr. d. Bremer Wiss. Gesellsch.*, 1930.

98 *Sermonis dator* according to an inscription on a statue in the Villa Albani, CIG. 5953, Farnell, *op. cit.*, p. 62.

98a Cf. E. Boisacq, *Dictionn. etym. de la langue grecque,* Heidelberg/Paris, 1923, p. 238.

99 Harpocrat. *s.v.*

100 At least since Sophocles. Cf. E. Kuhnert in Roscher, *op. cit.*, IV, p. 476.

101 On a vase painting, Hermes brings the child Dionysos to the old Silenos: Museo Gregoriano II, 26 in Roscher, *op. cit.*, p. 472.

102 E. Buschor, *Griechische Vasen*, Munich, 1940, p. 164, illus. 183f.

103 A. Dietrich, *Kleine Schriften*, Leipzig, 1911, p. 421.

104 Cf. L. Deubner, *Attische Feste*, Berlin, 1932, p. 112.

105 Buschor, *op. cit.*, p. 165, illus. 166f.

106 Cf. Kerényi, *Labyrinth-Studien,* Alb. Vigiliae XV, Amsterdam, 1941; *Werkausg.*, vol. I, pp. 226-273.

More on the Gods . . . .

The New Polytheism   by   *David L. Miller*
With wit and a wealth of evidence, Miller presents the current return to polytheism in religion, psychology, sociology, and the arts, thereby challenging theology to re-imagine itself. "His notions are tantalizing," said *Time.* "A book you dare not miss," declared *Le Monde* in Paris. With a Preface by Henry Corbin and James Hillman's "Psychology: Monotheistic or Polytheistic" extensively revised. (148 pages/ISBN 0-88214-314-X)

Dionysus: Myth and Cult   by   *Walter F. Otto*
An examination of Dionysiac worship in the maenad cults, the mask, tragedy and theatre, in silence, pandaemonium, and somber madness, through the vine and juices of vegetative nature, and in relation with woman, especially Ariadne. A full, authoritative phenomenology of the God by a rare scholar whose understanding carries the reader into participation. Plates, notes, index. (xxi, 243 pages/ISBN 0-88214-214-3)

An Anthology of Greek Tragedy
edited by   *Albert Cook and Edwin Dolin*
Eight major plays by Aeschylus, Sophocles, Euripides—each translated by contemporary published scholar-poets. A collection unique for its selection of texts and for its accuracy and beauty. Each play is introduced, and all have numbered lines for locating quotations. An excellent reference work—and a good read. Maps, theatre plans, bibliographies. (xl, 403 pages/ISBN 0-88214-215-1)

The Homeric Hymns   translated by   *Charles Boer*
Since 1972, this version of the *Homeric Hymns*—nominated for the National Book Award—has been acclaimed by critics and public and has widely established itself as a classroom text. These thirty-five poems are the earliest extant depiction of the Gods and Goddesses as individual figures. Boer's translation is a fresh and stunning experience, offering immediate access to the archetypal characters of the Greek pantheon. (vi, 182 pages/ISBN 0-88214-210-0)

Apollo: The Wind, the Spirit, and the God   by   *Karl Kerényi*
Apollo—a popular favorite among Greek deities and yet most misunderstood of divine concepts. Here is the original Apollo, a mysterious light-and-dark force revealed by the renowned psychological mythographer, Karl Kerényi. The four chapters examine Apollonian cult, myth, and thought, ranging through such disparate symbols as the serpents at Delphi, the broom of Ion, the swans of the *Phaedo*, and the winds of the North. (76 pages/ISBN 0-88214-216-X)

Pan and the Nightmare   by   *Wilhelm Roscher and James Hillman*
Roscher's monograph (the only translation in English) examines nightmare demons in Greek and Roman literature and discusses folklore, word origins, and ancient medical theories. Hillman's *An Essay on Pan* (translated into German and French and a bestseller in Italy) introduces Roscher and locates panic, rape, masturbation, nymphs in an archetypal psychology of Pan. Scholarly apparatus. (lxiii, 88 pages/ISBN 0-88214-204-6)

Spring Publications, Inc. • **P.O. Box 222069** • **Dallas, Texas 75222**